POETRY WORKSHOP FOR MIDDLE SCHOOL

Activities That Inspire Meaningful Language Learning

Michelle Ambrosini
Central Bucks School District
Doylestown, Pennsylvania, USA

Teresa M. Morretta
School District of Jenkintown
Jenkintown, Pennsylvania, USA

INTERNATIONAL
Reading Association
800 BARKSDALE ROAD, PO BOX 8139
NEWARK, DE 19714-8139, USA
www.reading.org

The International Reading Association attempts, through its publications, to provide a forum for a wide spectrum of opinions on reading. This policy permits divergent viewpoints without implying the endorsement of the Association.

Director of Publications   Joan M. Irwin
Editorial Director, Books and Special Projects   Matthew W. Baker
Managing Editor   Shannon Benner
Permissions Editor   Janet S. Parrack
Acquisitions and Communications Coordinator   Corinne M. Mooney
Associate Editor, Books and Special Projects   Sara J. Murphy
Assistant Editor   Charlene M. Nichols
Administrative Assistant   Michele Jester
Senior Editorial Assistant   Tyanna L. Collins
Production Department Manager   Iona Muscella
Supervisor, Electronic Publishing   Anette Schütz
Senior Electronic Publishing Specialist   Cheryl J. Strum
Electronic Publishing Specialist   R. Lynn Harrison
Proofreader   Elizabeth C. Hunt

Project Editor   Janet S. Parrack

Cover Design   Linda Steere

Web addresses in this book were correct as of the publication date but may have become inactive or otherwise modified since that time. If you notice a deactivated or changed Web address, please e-mail books@reading.org with the words "Website Update" in the subject line. In your message, specify the Web link, the book title, and the page number on which the link appears.

Library of Congress Cataloging-in-Publication Data
Ambrosini, Michelle.
    Poetry workshop for middle school : activities that inspire meaningful
language learning / Michelle Ambrosini, Teresa Morretta.
        p. cm.
Includes bibliographical references and index.
    ISBN 0-87207-517-6 (pbk. : alk. paper)
1. Poetry—Study and teaching (Middle school) I. Morretta, Teresa M.
II. Title.
    LB1575.A43 2003
    808.1'071'2—dc21

                                                                            2003012415

DEDICATION

Danielle, Nicole, & Michael Ambrosini—for letting me be the big sister

Sue Hanson—for being the best friend I always wanted

—Michelle

Louis Strupzcewski, my husband and soul mate—you complete me

Rosemary Morretta Weaver and Natalie Morretta Wojnar, my sisters—sisters by chance, friends by choice

Janine Giuliano, my lifelong friend—fate made us friends, but friendship makes us sisters

Dana Costanzo-White, my friend and soul grade partner—our connection as friends makes us better teachers

—Teresa

CONTENTS

PREFACE

As middle school teachers of reading and writing—Teresa for 21 years and Michelle for 10 years—we discuss our classroom practices and reflect on them, cognizant of national, state, and local standards. The result of our initial teacher inquiry was *Practical Approaches for Teaching Reading and Writing in Middle Schools* (2000). Further professional reading and discussions of what constitutes quality literacy instruction continue to fuel our reflections on instructional practices. This book, *Poetry Workshop for Middle School: Activities That Inspire Meaningful Language Learning*, is a synthesis of these reflections, which have made evident to us that poetry workshop supports meaningful language learning in middle school. We embrace and implement poetry workshop in our classrooms because students are immersed in reading and writing poetry, they learn and experience the benefits of revision in writing, and they show in their responses a progression from literal comprehension to critical analysis of text.

This book shows teachers, both novice and veteran, that poetry workshop is a means to "see how language excites" students (Esbensen, 1995, p. 5), while concurrently supporting local, state, and national standards. In the following chapters, we provide workshop activities that encourage adolescent writers to value their writing and the works of classic and contemporary poets. The activities focus on reading, writing, listening, and discussing poetry—providing opportunities for students to investigate their language. Poetry workshop is a component of a language arts classroom that values authentic audiences. In the workshop, students are readers who write poetry and writers who read poetry.

Chapter 1, "Laying a Foundation for Poetry Workshop," first defines poetry workshop and explains its value in the reading and writing classroom. We provide research to demonstrate that it is an effective practice for teachers of middle school students. By giving an overview of our combined approach to language arts instruction—the union of explicit instruction and whole language—we underscore how we engage middle school students *before* poetry workshop. We define some of the practical approaches for teaching reading and writing, including sustained silent reading (SSR), reader-response journals, literature circles, freewriting, and conferences. These literacy activities prepare students for poetry workshop because language learning is meaningful in a reading- and writing-rich environment that scaffolds students to make significant revisions in writing and to develop comprehension from the literal to the interpretative level.

For clarity, our design of poetry workshop is divided into three chapters—chapter 2, "Getting Started With Poetry Writing," chapter 3, "Diving Into Poetry Writing," and chapter 4, "Taking the Next Steps With Poetry Writing." We present the activities of poetry workshop in a user-friendly lesson plan, providing objectives, procedure or discussion, student samples, and select poems to be used in the activities. (Note: Poems or collections that are easily found are simply cited; poems that may not be as accessible are included.)

Chapter 2 provides initial activities that we implement to tap into students' background knowledge about poetry, to offer insight into poets' writing techniques, and to help students begin composing poetry.

In chapter 3, the activities build on students' learning in the beginning stages of poetry workshop. The activities yield a plethora of poetry-writing opportunities for students, encouraging their own writing styles to emerge and flourish.

Chapter 4 highlights what professional writers do and connects this process to poetry writing. This chapter also describes conferencing, revision, and publication—elucidating their importance for and impact on writers—and discusses assessment and its role in poetry workshop.

Chapter 5 is a compilation of poetry-writing activities—outside poetry workshop—that can be incorporated throughout the year and across the curriculum. In these activities, students respond to reading or communicate their knowledge in curricular areas by composing poems; now positioned as writers of poetry, they think critically about texts and their learning.

The appendixes provide instructional and learning resources for both teachers and students such as a poet's toolbox of types of poems and figures of speech, a list of mystery slips (nouns and adjectives), two graphic organizers, a rubric, an assessment tool, and three poems by well-known poets.

The purpose of poetry workshop is to engage students in making meaning of text as they read, write, listen to, and discuss poetry in a literacy-enriched environment. A true benefit of poetry workshop is that the teacher is able to engage all students in poetry writing, even the most reluctant writers. The format allows the teacher opportunities to work with individual students who may be plagued by writer's block. In our classrooms, we communicate to students that not every activity will ignite their creativity in the same way. For teachers to be full participants in the classroom community of readers and writers, we must share our strengths and weaknesses with students by modeling both our poems and our struggles with writer's block. This shared acknowledgment of struggling with the writing process, the format of poetry workshop, and the routine sharing of poetry writing among students in small-group and whole-class settings provide a comfort zone that engages students in quality literacy instruction.

MA and TMM

ACKNOWLEDGMENTS

Mom and Dad, my greatest teachers, I am grateful for your love, wisdom, and friendship. Grandmom Esterina and Grandmom Assunta—ti voglio bene. Nicole and Michael Ambrosini and Danielle and Scott Irvine, thank you for growing up with me. Sue and John Hanson, our friendship is one of "my favorite things." Jack, Brynne, and Mollie Hanson—cutest kids I know—thank you for laughs and hugs. Teresa Morretta, as a teacher and a friend, you are my role model. Tricia Adolph, you are my forever friend!

I appreciate the commitment to excellence in education of Nancy Silvious and Jason Bucher, Holicong Middle School principal and assistant principal, respectively. I am grateful to work with talented teachers, especially Mike Bartosweicz, Corinne Bennett, Allie Bowman, Bridget Collins, Jessica Dancu, Jim Glaser, Maryalice Hagan, Karl Hilbert, Patrick Kelly, Rita Kenefic, Aileen Kondyra, Lisa Levin, Beth Madden, Tricia Pfeil, Brooke Savage, and Bill Talley—you are true professionals.

My present and past students, thank you for sharing your writing and thinking with me. I have learned much from you.

—Michelle

Dad, Mom, and Grandmom, my memories of you color everything I do.

Joseph P. Morretta, I hope this isn't a step down for you from the dedication page! Joey, you have always been my "hero." To my nephews and nieces—Hugh and Matthew Morretta, Michael and Keri Weaver, Steven and Justin Strupczewski, and Katelyn Wojnar—you brighten my days. John Saunders, your lifelong love and friendship have helped shape me as a person. Michelle Ambrosini, professionally we connect—no doubt about it—but your love, talks, and ultimately your friendship add to my life. Hallee Adelman and Dave Seitz, your professional and personal examples constantly remind me to strive to be my best.

—Teresa

We appreciate Matt Baker and the guidance that he provided to us. His insight is amazing and has transformed our words into a stronger product.

CHAPTER 1

Laying a Foundation for Poetry Workshop

oetry workshop is a series of reading and writing activities, beginning in the reading and writing classroom and extending to other curricular areas. We design the poetry workshop as a three- to four-week plan whereby students, positioned as readers and writers, have daily sessions that immerse them in reading and writing poetry. Students meet as readers, writers, and listeners who exchange ideas, share writing, and hone techniques of poetry writing. In the workshop, students read poetry—their own and others'; students write poetry—personal and published; students listen to poetry—classics and classmates'; and students speak about poetry—as readers and writers. Reading, writing, and listening to poetry provide students with a foundation for discussions that propel them into meaningful transactions with text. The discussions that emerge expand students' interpretations of text, strengthening their critical thinking in the community of readers and writers.

In poetry workshop, students are both readers and writers, and the teacher is the facilitator. Students read published poets' writing, and the teacher makes explicit the tools that poets employ. The combination of authentic text and explicit teaching illustrates the classroom climate needed for meaningful language learning. Yet, although poetry workshop nourishes the growth of the community of readers and writers and makes visible the reading-writing connection, these ambitious goals are accomplished only after the foundation has been laid.

We established the foundation for the workshop by adopting a philosophy for teaching reading and writing that we call a combined approach. This approach embraces aspects of both explicit instruction and whole language—a complex blending beyond the scope of this book. In our experiences, this instructional approach has generated language learning that is meaningful and authentic and has created a community of readers and writers that possess the skills and concepts

necessary to achieve excellence (Morretta & Ambrosini, 2000). We acknowledge, however, that educators frequently choose either explicit instruction or whole language as the foundation of classroom instruction. Many educators view these philosophies as irreconcilable; however, our experience makes discernible that they are not.

Morrow and Tracey (1997) define explicit instruction as "the systematic, sequential presentation" of skills that uses "isolated, direct instructional strategies" (p. 646). Explicit instruction equips students with factual knowledge of concepts and skills; however, alone and without regard to the use of these skills in the real world, explicit instruction discourages meaningful learning. Yatvin (1991) explains that whole language is "the belief that language learning depends on the learner's self-confidence and integration of real language use into learning activities" (p. 2). Whole language promotes meaningful learning because it employs authentic texts and respects students' interests and prior knowledge; however, it may leave gaps in language learning if skills and concepts are not attended to in a sequence that is developmentally appropriate for learners. Explicit instruction and whole language are combined successfully when a teacher understands that, for language learning to be effective, elements of both should coexist.

A teacher generates visible changes in the classroom when he or she adopts a combined approach as his or her language-learning philosophy. Teachers create activities in which students practice and study language in ways that are closely related to how they will use it in the real world. Choices of various texts and genres—contemporary works, classics, fiction, nonfiction, poetry, and picture books—not only enrich students' experiences with literature, but also invest them in their learning. Conversations surface about books—book talks, literature circles, and response groups—that are focused by the teacher but led by the students, and that mirror real-world discourse about books. Daily reading and writing—sustained silent reading (SSR), freewriting, and teacher modeling of reading and writing—support students' growth as effective communicators. Language instruction, focusing on conventions and skills, incorporates real literature to show how authors use writing skills and language conventions. The classroom dynamics that emerge demonstrate the combined approach.

Next in this chapter, we provide a short synopsis of some teaching and learning practices that enliven the combined approach. These instructional practices—what we term *practical approaches*—prepare our students to transact with and compose poetry in poetry workshop. These practical approaches, which support what researchers purport is fundamental to language learning, create a bustling classroom in which students read, write, conference, and critically think about self, others, and the world.

For clarity, we now consider the reading and the writing aspects of poetry workshop separately, although we acknowledge and affirm that these processes occur concurrently. We provide support from research for each aspect and a description of each aspect in action, giving a picture of the reading and writing classroom during poetry workshop. We also offer an overview of the practical approaches that we have adopted in poetry workshop to create a community of readers who write and writers who read. Students, once they become actively involved in this community, are primed to celebrate the reading-writing connection.

The Reading Aspect of Poetry Workshop

Support From Research

In *Literature as Exploration*, Rosenblatt (1995) states, "A novel or poem or play remains merely inkspots on paper until a reader transforms them into a set of meaningful symbols" (p. 24). To create proficient readers and writers, the teacher's task is to implement literacy activities that position students to transact with the text to make meaning, immersing them in a literacy-enriched environment. During poetry workshop, the teacher provides opportunities for students to move in and out of the aesthetic and efferent stances (Rosenblatt, 1995). Students read poetry for enjoyment—taking the aesthetic stance—and they read poetry critically, noting how poets engage readers—taking the efferent stance. Rosenblatt (1995) explains, "Both cognitive and affective elements are present in all reading" (p. xvi–xvii). Poetry workshop honors both elements, encouraging students to be reflective while reading—analyzing, interpreting, and connecting with the text.

Zemelman, Daniels, and Hyde (1998) identify and define the qualities of best practice of literacy instruction, basing their conclusions on highly regarded documents such as the *Standards for the English Language Arts* (International Reading Association & National Council of Teachers of English, 1996), *Becoming a Nation of Readers: The Report of the Commission on Reading* (National Institute of Education, 1985), *New Policy Guidelines for Reading* (Harste, 1989), and the *National Board Standards* (National Board for Professional Teaching Standards, 2001). Zemelman et al. (1998) recommend and explain good literacy instruction, which includes the following practices: reading aloud, allowing time for independent reading, allowing student choice, providing exposure to a wide and rich range of literature, combining social and collaborative activities with much discussion and interaction, following silent reading with discussion, and teaching skills in the context of unabridged and meaningful literature. These recommended practices are alive in poetry workshop.

Reading in the Poetry Workshop

During poetry workshop, an extensive assortment of poetry texts is available for students to read during SSR and reading/writing workshop (time allotted for students to read, write, or work on their portfolios). The teacher reads aloud poems, and students are required to bring to class collections of poetry that they share aloud as well. The "living poetry anthology" is created on a classroom bulletin board by students, teachers, and administrators who are invited to post favorite poems for others to experience. Clearly, in this literacy-enriched environment, students read independently, make choices that allow for ownership of their learning, and are engaged in the meaning-making process of reading.

A key literacy activity of poetry workshop is poet study, in which literature circles are designed to have students coconstruct meaning by analyzing and interpreting poetry texts in discussions. Each student becomes an expert on either a classic or contemporary poet, reading the collection of poems independently or with others. By actively reading and taking notes to amass comments, questions, and reflections, students analyze poets' use of literary devices—figurative language, placement of lines and words, and choice of titles. Thus, students become cognizant of how poets engage readers. After transacting with the texts, students participate in literature circle meetings. In these "grand conversations" (Peterson & Eeds, 1990), students have opportunities to extend and elaborate on their individual understandings of a text. They share their critical reflections, coconstructing meaning and sparking interest in other classic or contemporary poets. Individually and collaboratively, students have read, analyzed, and interpreted poetry—making meaning from the written word.

One session of poetry workshop involves students reading a teacher-selected poem. Students record their reactions and connections to the words of the poem. Using their interpretations, students create their own poems, encapsulating their personal responses. When reading their own poems aloud and after listening to their classmates' poems, students respond, guided by questions from *The Reading/Writing Teacher's Companion: Explore Poetry* (Graves, 1992; see chapter 4, page 51, of this book). These questions help students to respond critically about another's writing—describing a poet's use of literary devices that create images for the listener or noting the poet's arrangement of lines to procure a desired effect for the reader. In all responses, students substantiate their opinions, citing the poem's words or structure. Taking the aesthetic and efferent stances, students read and respond to poems, making meaning through reading, analyzing, interpreting, connecting, speaking, and listening.

Practical Approaches for Reading

As veteran participants in a dynamic learning environment, many students move naturally into poetry workshop because they are accustomed to experiencing and responding to literature and writing for readers in ways closely related to how they will encounter language in the real world—making meaning from text, critically thinking about language, and communicating in written form. Several practical approaches implemented in the reading and writing classroom lay the foundation for poetry workshop: SSR, reader-response journals, literature circles, freewriting, and conferencing.

Sustained Silent Reading (SSR). This is a block of time at the beginning or end of the class period that allows students opportunities to read their own choices for pleasure and shows students that a purpose for reading is enjoyment, which serves the goal of developing lifelong readers. Once SSR becomes a daily ritual of the reading and writing classroom, students eagerly anticipate this time to read. Students value reading, making it easy for the teacher to lead them to transact with text: connecting, evaluating, and elaborating meaning. Poetry reading during poetry workshop then is a natural and enriching experience for students because reading is habitual for them and critical response to texts is second nature.

Reader-Response Journals. Students use these journals, namely dialogue journals and double-entry journals, to record their responses to literature; they reflect on text and make their personal meaning visible. The dialogue journal about reading—written dialogue between students and the teacher or peers about something that they have read recently—illustrates the power of dialogue, a living conversation, to make and communicate personal meaning. A double-entry journal, in which students divide their pages into two columns, writing summaries on the left and personal reflections on the right, is a tangible sign that students are experiencing and responding to literature: summarizing and analyzing the text by connecting it to their own lives, noticing similarities with other texts, questioning characters' motives or identifying with characters, and noting an author's use of language. Through the use of reader-response journals, students practice reading between the lines, moving beyond literal comprehension, and they also voice this critical thinking in writing. Now, in poetry workshop, students are engaged, active participants, able to glean deeper meaning from a writer's words and to become poets who make decisions about their writing based on their awareness of their readers.

Literature Circles. These are small groups in which students meet to discuss their interpretations of texts; these discussions expand on their meaning of text and build their comprehension by including the varied interpretations of others. The meaning that a student makes about a text is elaborated on by others' insights. Students are given opportunities to reconcile their own interpretations with those of their literature circle members, which fosters critical thinking. Literature circles prime students for listening and responding to peers in a constructive manner. The discussion of and reflection on poetry—published poets and classroom poets—are integral to poetry workshop.

The Writing Aspect of Poetry Workshop

Support From Research

Positioned as writers who read, students compose poetry during poetry workshop to make personal meaning and communicate with an audience. As students write in poetry workshop, they reveal their personal experiences. Student writing is enriched by what Rosenblatt (1995) terms "lived through" experiences (p. 33). Students participate in the writing process for authentic purposes, using what they have discovered about the characteristics of quality writing, the poetry genre, and the English language. Poetry workshop encourages students to be reflective, engaging them in the recursive process of writing in which they compose, revise, and edit their poems independently and collaboratively. Student writing created during poetry workshop evinces that they have made meaning of language.

In *A Fresh Look at Writing*, Graves (1994) endorses the following teacher actions that are fundamental to engaging students in the recursive nature of the writing process, specifically the poetry genre:

> help children read the world for sources of poems to write (p. 328)
>
> respond to children's poetry (p. 335)
>
> read other poets aloud to the children (p. 337)
>
> help children to practice evaluating their own work and the work of professional writers (p. 138)

Zemelman et al. (1998) identify the qualities of best practice in teaching writing and highlight the main characteristics and strategies of an effective writing program, based on the following resources: *Research on Written Composition* (Hillocks, 1986), *Standards for the English Language Arts* (IRA/NCTE, 1996), and the *Standards in Practice* series (NCTE, 1996). Zemelman et al. recommend that writing teachers incorporate the following best practices, which are embodied in poetry workshop:

student ownership; classroom time spent on writing whole and original pieces; instruction in and support for all stages of writing process; teacher modeling all stages of writing process; teaching grammar and mechanics in context; writing for real audiences; publishing for the class and wider communities; active exchange and valuing of students' ideas; collaborative small-group work; conferences and peer critiquing that give responsibility for improvement to the authors; brief, informal oral responses as students work; and encouragement of risk taking and honest expression. (1998, p. 82)

Writing in the Poetry Workshop

To provide a scaffold for students, poetry writing in the workshop begins with a minilesson that familiarizes students with literary devices—alliteration, simile, metaphor, personification, onomatopoeia, hyperbole, and repetition—that published poets employ to engage readers. Another minilesson focuses on various forms of poetry—free verse, narrative, lyric, and found—followed by examples from contemporary and classic poets. Once they are familiar with literary devices and poetry types and can reference models of these, students are ready to become writers who compose texts, constructing and communicating meaning with the written word. Then, teachers implement numerous literacy activities that inspire student writers. These activities, explained in the following chapters, are the heart of poetry workshop—engaging students to make meaning through composing poems.

Once students are immersed in poetry writing, the goal is to strengthen this skill. Literacy minilessons focusing on revision—taking a second look at writing—take precedence at this workshop stage. Revision, a major component of the recursive writing process, is intensified when contemporary and classic and student and teacher poetry are used as models. In these lessons, students learn how poets manipulate lines, words, punctuation, rhyme, repetition, titles, and organizational elements to communicate meaning to a reader. Minilessons also hone students' understanding of the English language. For example, the teacher initiates a discussion about using strong verbs as a technique to create an image for a reader. As engaged, active participants in the recursive writing process, student writers are empowered to experiment and take risks with language—creating meaningful writing for themselves and others.

Practical Approaches for Writing

Freewriting.   This is time set aside at the beginning or end of a class period that allows students opportunities to write about topics of their choice. This activity demonstrates that writing is valuable because the teacher models the approach and designates class time for it. The teacher also writes and then shares the writing with the class; likewise, students are encouraged to share their freewriting by reading aloud. Teachers can highlight some characteristics of good writing during the sharing of freewriting examples. Once freewriting has become a regular component of the reading and writing classroom, students are comfortable writing and more willing to share their writing with others. This practical approach readies students to compose texts and share their poems during poetry workshop.

Conferencing. This is a conversation about text that takes place between a student writer and a teacher or peer. It is a social practice with the goal of improving not only the written piece but also the writer. Conferencing illustrates to students that they and their writing are valuable because the teacher and students' peers give individual attention to them and their writing. Students become further invested in their writing because a real audience is anticipated. As a result of conferencing, students are empowered to take a second look at their writing, make choices about their use of language, and think critically about how and what they are communicating to readers, which continues the recursive writing process. This practical approach makes tangible to student writers that revision plays a significant role in communicating to readers. As students compose their own poems in poetry workshop, they are comfortable with conferencing and are cognizant of its value for written communication.

Students who have been engaged in such literacy activities, which position them as authentic readers and writers, are ripe to practice their experiences in the poetry genre, making poetry another conduit for meaningful reading and writing.

The next two chapters focus on activities to engross students in poetry writing. In chapter 2, the activities introduce students to the poetry genre, building their comfort level. The activities in chapter 3 further propel students to write poetry that is in tune with their senses while reflecting their unique writing styles and communicating ideas about their world.

CHAPTER 2

Getting Started With Poetry Writing

The activities in this chapter illustrate how poetry workshop eases students into poetry writing. We implement the activities to debunk some of the myths that students hold about poetry, to teach techniques that poets employ to engage readers, and to build students' confidence and comfort levels with writing poetry. The initial sessions of poetry workshop spark an interest and enthusiasm in student writers—even those who are usually reluctant.

To begin each session of poetry workshop, the teacher reads aloud a favorite poem for students to listen to and enjoy. Students also bring books of poetry to read during sustained silent reading (SSR), immersing themselves in a poetry-rich environment. Eventually, students select poems to read aloud to the whole class, strengthening the community of readers and writers who listen to and enjoy poetry.

Another way to begin students' experiences with the poetry genre is the living poetry anthology, which we adopted from Georgia Heard's (1999) *Awakening the Heart: Exploring Poetry in Elementary and Middle School*. On a designated bulletin board, students and other members of the school community—principal, teachers, librarian, and parents—are invited to post copies of favorite poems. This living poetry anthology sparks in students an excitement about reading poetry, resulting in impromptu poetry discussions. Poetry comes alive because students initiate conversations about it in a social setting with other students, apart from the teacher.

With activities such as SSR and the living poetry anthology, teachers have positioned students to transact with poetry in informal ways, easing their entry into studying the genre. The activities in this chapter make learning about poetry concrete for students by expanding their knowledge of poetry, providing a toolbox of writing techniques, and scaffolding their writing with specified formats that ensure success.

ACTIVITY 1   Poetry Is...

Objectives
- To activate students' prior knowledge of poetry
- To debunk myths that students have about poetry
- To build student confidence for poetry writing

Procedure

To acknowledge students' preconceived ideas about what poetry is or is not, they individually make a web, listing words and phrases that they associate with poetry. Next, students share their ideas within a small group. Finally, the whole class discusses the responses, which are then displayed.

From our experiences, the most common student responses are that poems rhyme, are short in length, and adhere to a prescribed format such as cinquain, haiku, or limerick. The teacher's task is to demonstrate that poetry ranges from prescribed formats to free verse, uses language in unconventional ways, and is written for personal reasons or for an audience.

To demonstrate that poetry may be unrhymed and may use dialect, the teacher displays "Mother to Son" by Langston Hughes (see chapter 4, page 53). To counter the misconception that poems are short, the teacher shares Henry Wadsworth Longfellow's "Paul Revere's Ride"—a lengthy poem that recounts a historical event.

The teacher also highlights less familiar styles of poetry, such as those with more than one voice. For example, in the Newbery Medal book *Joyful Noise: Poems for Two Voices*, Paul Fleischman (1988) writes a collection of poems that feature two voices or speakers. Each poem is presented in two columns, side by side on the page (see chapter 5, page 88). A variation of this format appears in the poem "Conversation With a Kite" by Bobbi Katz, which features dialogue between a child and a kite. The lines of both speakers are read separately, alternating between the child and the kite and indicated by italics.

The teacher discusses with students that poets write with different audiences in mind. For example, the teacher shares some background about Emily Dickinson, who wrote poetry in the early 1800s purely for personal expression, which "Poem 27: I'm Nobody! Who Are You?" illustrates (see page 12). An illustrative juxtaposition is "No Grown-ups" by Shel Silverstein (see page 13), a modern poet who clearly wrote this poem with children as his intended audience.

Wrapping Up

The previous session makes clear to students that as writers of poetry they are not mandated to follow any poetry rules. As students gain greater insight into poetry, they become more willing to take risks as writers.

Conversation With a Kite

Come back, come back, my runaway kite!
Come back and play with me!
I'm riding and gliding on whirl-away winds.
I'm going somewhere. Can't you see?
Where are you going, my beautiful kite,
flying so high in the sky?
I'm going to visit the lost balloons
that made little children cry.
When I hold your string, oh my magical kite,
why do I feel the wind in my hand?
The wind is a taste of the sky, my young friend,
that I give to a child of the land.

—BOBBI KATZ

I'm Nobody! Who Are You?

I'm nobody! Who are you?
Are you nobody, too?
Then there's a pair of us—don't tell!
They'd banish us, you know.

How dreary to be somebody!
How public, like a frog
To tell your name the livelong day
To an admiring bog!

—EMILY DICKINSON

No Grown-ups

No grown-ups allowed.
We're playin' a game,
And we don't need
"Be carefuls" or "don'ts."
No grown-ups allowed.
We're formin' a club,
And the secret oath
Must not be shown.
No grown-ups allowed.
We're goin' for pizza—
No, no one but me and my crowd.
So just stay away.
Oh, now it's time to pay?
Grown-ups allowed.

—Shel Silverstein

From Silverstein, S. (1996). Falling Up. Used by permission of HarperCollins Publishers.

Objectives
• To familiarize students with the figures of speech that poets use to create images for a reader
• To familiarize students with the types of poems that poets write

Procedure
Poets frequently write different types of poems and employ figures of speech to engage readers. This activity introduces students to the Poet's Toolbox (see Appendix A), a list of literary devices and poetry styles for student writers to use in their poetry writing.

The teacher discusses figures of speech such as metaphor, simile, hyperbole, personification, alliteration, onomatopoeia, repetition, and imagery, and types of poetry such as lyric, free verse, and narrative poetry. The teacher's task is to illustrate and highlight the power of these figures of speech and types of poetry and how they are used to create images for readers. This activity makes it clear to students how these devices make a difference in their writing.

In our classrooms, we use "Scale" by Shel Silverstein to illustrate hyperbole and simile, and for onomatopoeia and repetition we use the picture book *The Little Old Woman and the Hungry Cat* by Nancy Polette (1989).

To illustrate different types of poetry, the teacher reads "Stopping by Woods on a Snowy Evening" by Robert Frost and *The Napping House*, a picture book by Audrey Wood (1984), as examples of lyric poetry. Examples of narrative poetry include "Paul Revere's Ride" by Longfellow, "Casey at the Bat" by Edmund Thayer, and *Lady Bugatti*, a picture book by Joyce Maxner (1991).

Wrapping Up
The Poet's Toolbox provides definitions and examples for students to use as a reference while they compose their poetry. Activity 2 builds on Activity 1, showing students that there are no definite poetry rules. Students become more comfortable with experimenting with language as they learn the literary devices used by poets and become more familiar with various types of poems. The Poet's Toolbox becomes a safety net for hesitant writers and a geyser of ideas for more confident ones. Teachers may want to consult the many available literature anthologies, which often contain sections that address the teaching of poetry and literary devices.

Scale

If I could only see the scale,

I'm sure that it would state

That I've lost ounces...maybe pounds

Or even tons of weight.

"You'd better eat some pancakes—

You're skinny as a rail."

I'm sure that's what the scale would say...

If I could see the scale.

—SHEL SILVERSTEIN

From Silverstein, S. (1996). Falling Up. Used by permission of HarperCollins Publishers.

Objectives
• To compose poetry that personifies a place, thing, or idea
• To compose poetry that follows a specified format

Procedure
Poetry activities that employ specified formats, such as haiku, cinquian, and dia-mante, vary in the degree to which they scaffold writers' responses. This activity depends greatly on prewriting and drafting formats (Figure 1) to achieve personifi-cation, which conveys images that use all the senses. Because this activity follows specified formats, reluctant writers are more successful because the risks that they feel as writers are lessened. A typical complaint of reluctant writers is "I don't know where to start." This activity serves as the impetus that they need to begin writing.

    To implement this activity, the following teacher-written poem is used as a model for students. Because the benefits of teacher modeling extend to every as-pect of learning, this is an excellent, nonthreatening opportunity to offer students a view of teachers as writers.

Traffic Jam
I saw Traffic Jam clearly.
She was a tall aluminum rainbow.
She lay motionless, lurched forward slightly,
    and blinked scarlet red.
I saw her transparent eyes that held the sun
And heard her honking fits and smoky sighs
And I felt as irritated as an itchy mosquito bite.

—MICHELLE AMBROSINI

    After reading aloud a poem, the teacher explains how a poet can use the prewriting and drafting formats as the first step in composing a poem (see Figure 1). These formats provide a safety net for the student writer just as they do for the teacher writer.

    The prewriting and drafting formats scaffold the following students' beginning steps with poetry writing, focusing on the use of personification. Both students ad-here strictly to the formats, yet they create distinct images, communicating their in-terpretations of jealousy and homework to readers.

```
┌─────────────────────────────────────────────────────────────────┐
│                     F I G U R E   1                             │
│              Prewriting and Drafting Formats                     │
│ Prewriting: Fill in the description of the person who you have imagined. │
│ 1. What you are representing as a person:_____ │
│ 2. The person's body type:_____ │
│ 3. How the person moves:_____ │
│ 4. The person's coloring (hair, eyes):_____ │
│ 5. How the person speaks:_____ │
│ 6. How the person makes you feel:_____ │
│                                                                  │
│ Drafting: Copy the format and fill in your responses from above. │
│ I saw _____(1)_____ clearly.  │
│ He/She was _____(2)_____. │
│ He/She _____(3)_____ , _____(3)_____ , and _____(3)_____.   │
│ I saw his/her _____(4)_____.  │
│ And heard him/her _____(5)_____.  │
│ And I felt _____(6)_____.  │
└─────────────────────────────────────────────────────────────────┘
```

Jealousy

I saw Jealousy clearly,
She was tall and lean.
She turned into the light, her sallow skin illuminated.
I saw her sunken eyes black as coal,
And heard her syrupy voice, fluid, as it flooded my ears
And I felt the fire in her eyes.

—LUIS, AGE 12

Homework

I saw Homework clearly.
He was a giant binder, exploding at the seam with mounds of
    paper.
He turned, quick and sneaky, and slid into my book bag.
I saw his bright white, blue lined skin and questioning ink-black
    eyes,
And heard him laugh and shout questions, demanding
    answers.
And I felt as overwhelmed as when I have to clean my room.

—JULIE, AGE 12

Wrapping Up

After composing drafts using the formats, students conference about their drafts in small groups and as a whole class. Conferencing about narrative, informational, and persuasive writing, and literature circle discussions (see chapter 1) have laid the foundation for students to respond to peers' writing in meaningful ways, so the next step—conferencing about poetry writing—occurs naturally in our classrooms. However, after the first poetry-writing activity moves through the drafting stage and most students have a work in progress, it may be necessary for the teacher to present a minilesson on how to listen and respond to another's writing (see chapter 4).

Small-group and whole-class conferencing about student writing is repeated in each activity. It should be understood that conferencing occurs among the students after drafting, even if we do not explicitly state this fact as a part of the procedure for an activity.

Objectives
• To compose poetry that elicits personal interpretation of ordinary objects
• To compose poetry that follows a specified format

Procedure
As students read and write poetry in poetry workshop, they inevitably begin to model their writing on the works of other poets. The following poem is the teaching tool for this activity.

Sneakers
Laced,
Shiny, and
Leather-scented,
Poised on display

Sneakers leap,
pounce, and
twist
on the inky
cold cement

Now they
slump
unlaced, scuffed, and
sock-infested
in a corner of a closet

—MICHELLE AMBROSINI

The before-and-after poem consists of three stanzas. The first stanza lists four descriptive words or phrases about the topic. The second stanza, written as lines of poetry, describes the topic in its "before" state. The third stanza describes the topic in its "after" state.

After reading the poem aloud, the teacher discusses the format of each stanza. The first stanza—"laced," "shiny," "leather-scented," and "poised on display"—introduces the topic "sneakers" to the reader. The second stanza describes the sneakers before—"Sneakers leap, pounce, and twist on the inky cold cement." The third stanza describes the sneakers after—"Now they slump, unlaced, scuffed, and sock-infested in a corner of a closet."

Students draft for approximately 15 to 20 minutes about various topics of their choice using the three-stanza model "Sneakers." The teacher reminds students while writing to think about what may have transpired to cause the change from *before* to *after*. This prepares students to delve deeper into the topics that they choose to write about, influencing the words and images chosen. Students conference in small groups and as a whole class.

Wrapping Up

The following student poetry demonstrates the power of this activity as students write about ordinary objects fueled by their imaginations, while entertaining and engaging readers. In relatively few lines, students tell a story whose impact is strengthened by its concise structure. For example, in the following poems, students create images in each stanza that compel the reader to transact with the text. The reader imagines details that move the narrative from the second (before) stanza to the third (after) stanza.

The Skateboard
Fast
Smooth
Awesome
Agile

The skateboard flies
Hops
Spins so quick

Now it sits
In the trash
Scratched
Bashed
Awkward

—Ryan, age 12

Nail Polish
Smelly
Bright
Wet
Smooth

The nail polish
Strokes
Over the fingernail

Dry
Now this paint
A pretty shield of plastic

—Arielle, age 12

Peanut

Salty
Hard
Oval shape
Brown

Lying in a bag
Waiting
At the park
To be sold

Now
It is cracked
Open to the day
Down the throat
And into
The dead
Dark
Stomach

—Matthew, age 12

Now that students' myths about poetry are debunked and they have a toolbox of techniques to use and greater confidence in themselves as poets, they are prepared and eager to dive into poetry writing. Although the activities in this chapter scaffold student poets, the activities in chapter 3 inspire and engage students to write poetry in a less guided fashion.

Diving Into Poetry Writing

In the initial activities of poetry workshop, students compose and share their poems. The activities in the previous chapters introduce students to poetry writing within set parameters. Primed to move beyond the format type of poetry writing, students are engaged and inspired to write poetry in novel ways. Students compose poems inspired by their senses and imaginations, music, and words. The activities in this chapter position students to make and communicate personal meaning, to recognize the power of the written word, and to compose poems to reflect their unique writing styles.

ACTIVITY 5   Music

Objective
• To compose poetry that makes personal meaning of musical selections

Procedure
In *With a Poet's Eye: Children Translate the World*, McVeigh-Schultz and Ellis (1997) discuss music as a means to inspire children to write poetry. Music motivates students to think beyond the composer's message, making personal meaning when writing poetry.

We selected "Pass the Peas" by The J.B's; "Trainspotting" by Primal Scream; "Symphony No. 9, Song of Joy" by Beethoven; "Fascinating Rhythm" by George Gershwin; "Sabre Dance" by Khachaturian; "The Nutcracker, Dance of the Sugar-Plum Fairy" by Tchaikovsky; and "Rhapsody in Blue" by George Gershwin. We find that musical choices that are primarily instrumental are best because lyrics may interfere with students' original thoughts.

McVeigh-Schultz and Ellis suggest playing each musical selection twice. The first time that a selection is played, students close their eyes, becoming attuned to all five senses. The teacher asks probing questions, focusing students on their senses. Eventually, a teacher's experience with facilitating poetry workshop will shape the questions posed. The following questions can be used to begin the inquiry:

- Where are you, and what scents do you associate with this place?
- What season is it when this music is playing?
- Who is dancing to this music, and how do they move?
- What color does this music remind you of?
- What animal does the music move like?
- What taste does the music make you think of?

The second time the musical selection is played, students jot down words and phrases while the teacher repeats the probing questions. After this process is repeated for each musical selection, students draft poems inspired by this brainstorm. Students can combine words, ideas, and images from all musical selections into one poem, or they can compose separate poems for each tune. Once drafting is completed, conferencing follows.

In the following student examples, it is clear that the students have made personal meaning. They access the Poet's Toolbox (see Appendix A) to help create images by employing metaphor, simile, alliteration, repetition, and onomatopoeia. In the first poem, the student has written a free verse poem, arranging the lines and stanzas to communicate to the reader. In the second poem, the student has extended a metaphor, likening the elements of spring to an orchestra.

The Deep Music Sea

Music is deep
as deep as the soul.
Music is fuel
fuel for the soul.
We dance about the room
swinging with a partner
shimmying across the floor.
I move, move, move.
I hop
bop
dance to the music.
Down a sunny street
I play my horn
the trumpet
its sound fills the air.

Music is deep
as deep as the soul.
I lurk
around the jungle
circling as I walk
making sure
I'm no one's dinner.
But now
I find myself
on a small stage.
Someone plays the bongos
behind me.
I move, move, move
to the groove of the music.

Music is deep
as deep as the soul.
Maybe deeper.
I swing, swing, swing
in my bright red dress
in the big concert hall.
I move
I groove
I swing
The music ends.
I have surfaced
from the deep music sea.

—MALIA, AGE 12

Springtime Orchestra

Stepping outside,
Into the spring auditorium,
The conducting trees,
Start the beautiful music,
As the wind whistles the tune,
The grass takes their solo,
Sitting down,
They join the buzzing of the bees,
The birds cut in,
And make up their own melody,
The clouds cry,
And blow flowers up on their stage,
As the sun applauds,
They start another song,
In the springtime orchestra

—CHRISTOPHER, AGE 11

In the next two student poems, the students also make personal meaning, but while the previous poems are explicitly connected to the music, the following poems inspire the students in a different way. One student connects the music to the circus, and one describes a fantastic encounter between man and beast.

La Nouba [The Party]

Red, white and blue
Dancing, singing, and music
Men and women in colorful costumes
Magical
Trapeze artists, tight rope walking and
Trampolines
Clowns that are funny
And men that yell
Running and weird walking
A spectacle
Cirque de Soleil

—MICHAEL, AGE 12

Drumbeats

Boom Boom
The tiger pounces
Faster than the eye can follow
Boom   Boom
The man leaps forward, his knife at the ready
Boom   Boom   Boom
The two collide
Boom
With a deafening roar of anger
The tiger leaps forward
This time grappling with the man
Boom   Boom
The knife's knocked out of the man's hand
Boom   Boom   Boom   Boom
Slowly the King of Cobras slithers between
The two jungle warriors
Hssss   Sah!
The serpent king strikes, quick as lightning
But the man is quicker

He hurls the snake
The snake slithers away

Defeat registers on the snake's face
In a deadly dance the tiger and the man circle
Around each other
Waiting for a chance
Boom   Boom
Thud
For the second time the tiger pounces
Landing on the man
Boom   Boom   Boom
The man grabs his last knife
Boom   Boom   Boom
The tiger is
No more
Boom
But the man is not the winner
The serpent's poison creeps through
The man's body
The man falls
Never to rise again
Somewhere the snake hisses
In triumph
Hssss   Sah!

—JOSHUA, AGE 11

In the next two examples, both students are inspired by music to write about dreams using unique images.

Dreamer

I close my eyes and take a breath
And find myself in the ocean's depth
I see a shark I better run
I think I used up all my fun

I close my eyes and take a breather
And find myself in Jungle fever
I start to dance, dance around
As I boogie to the jungle sound

An elephant stomps,
A cricket chirps,
I think I heard a lion burp

I close my eyes and take a sigh
And now I'm wondering why
Is it false or is it true?
I think it's all up to you
Now back to sleep to lay down my head
All snuggled up in my quiet bed.

—ARIELLE, AGE 11

Music World

Walking through the cold New York street
A jazz band I encounter
I close my eyes and start to dance
Until his saxophone gets louder
I open my eyes only to see
An elephant trumpeting his nose at me
I fall back and the ground is cold
Then I see them, young and old.
The ballerinas yell at me
And then they all start to scream.
Then I head it, crack, crack, crack
And I fall 'til there's a pain in my back
I awake on the floor next to my bed
But that Music World won't leave my head.

—BRITTANY, AGE 11

Wrapping Up

In our experiences, even the most reluctant writers have produced poems that convey the personal meaning of music. The musical selections are carefully chosen to include various genres and sounds, fostering interpretations as diverse as the students themselves. As shown in the preceding examples, music is a powerful medium that can be used to inspire students' poetry writing.

ACTIVITY 6   Mystery Slips

Objectives
• To compose poetry by positioning pairs of words in unique ways
• To compose poetry that moves writers beyond literal word meaning

Procedure
In *A Celebration of Bees: Helping Children Write Poetry*, Barbara Juster Esbensen (1995) describes the use of "mystery slips" (p. 250) as a means to inspire students to write poetry. Mystery slips are nouns and adjectives (see Appendix B), written on slips of paper that students select randomly, which appear side by side, at least once, in a poem. This activity encourages students to have fun with words and take risks as poets, inviting them to see ordinary objects in completely different ways.

The teacher fills two containers with words—one container holds nouns written on colored paper and the other holds adjectives written on a different colored paper. The mystery slips generate thinking and writing that go beyond a word's denotation, and the poems that students write using mystery slips vary from silly to serious. We include unfamiliar words to enrich students' vocabularies and familiar words that they are studying in class to expand their understanding and usage of the words.

Students choose one slip from each container. The two words must appear side by side at least once in the student's poem. First, the teacher models the process by choosing a word from each container and writing the two words together on a transparency or chart paper. The students observe the teacher engaged in the writing process. Another way to model this activity is to use the following student example or one from your own students. The mystery slip choice "dazzling diamonds," an example of alliteration, triggers the student's use of alliteration throughout her poem:

Glitter
high up in the jet blue sky
the sun
sparkles
down
an array of lovely colors
gives a sense of awe
gorgeous green
rambunctious red

vivid violet
yearning yellow
ornery orange
beautiful blue
intoxicated indigo
dazzling diamonds
sparkling sunlight
shimmering like silk
glitter
glitter
glitter

—JENNIE, AGE 12

In the following student examples, seemingly unrelated words (see bold face) inspire critical thinking and stretch writers' imaginations. In the first poem, the student uses personification to create an image for the reader. In the second poem, the student creates a metaphor that compares a jewel to soap.

My Agitated Dress

My **agitated dress** is mean
You see
It rips and tears and then it trips
Me
I am mad at my **agitated dress**
I am mad
Yes, oh . . .
YES!

—BRYN, AGE 11

Sudsy Emeralds

Sudsy emeralds
Colorful, sparkling
Ivy soap
Glossy
Floating
Greenish bubbles
Bright

Smooth
Sudsy emeralds

—ERIN, AGE 12

At times students may select mystery slips that have obvious connections, such as "chaotic lunchroom" in the following poem. In this poem, the student's personal experiences and imagination shape the poem, and he also uses onomatopoeia to create images for the reader.

The Chaotic Lunchroom

Chit, Chat,
Food Fight,
The teacher's nightmare,
A **chaotic lunchroom**,
Where everyone's wild,
They scream and tease and never stop,
Food in the air,
Everyone stares,
It hits a kid,
Who falls to the ground,
Mashed potatoes on the ground,
Whipped cream pies on people's faces,
SPLAT!
Uh-oh, it hit the principal!

—KEITH, AGE 11

In the following poems, the mystery slips (see bold face) inspire students to write about ordinary subjects such as the beach or a window, attaching a significance deeper than expected.

A Day at the Beach

Warm, soft sand
Wraps around my feet
Waves of joy make my heart beat
Winding colors of the sun tickle the sky pink

Blue clear water glistens in the sun
Palm trees whistle a soothing tune
The cool breeze calms the heat

The happiness of the moon starts the night
How long will I stay in this paradise?

—KATIE, AGE 12

Golden Windows

The magical **golden windows**
Can make all your dreams come true.
All you must do is wish your hardest
And then you must step through.

The golden window can change your life
It can change it good or bad.
The golden window can change your life
It can make it happy or sad.

If you ever pass by a golden window
Be sure to make a wish.
You can wish for anything
From a golden dog to a fancy dish.

—KRISTIN, AGE 11

Wrapping Up

As poetry workshop continues, small-group and whole-class writing conferences make students cognizant that they are writing for an audience and that the details in their writing engage that audience. Because of conferencing, writers not only revise during drafting but also continue to revise as they finalize their writing. Often, after students share their writing aloud, we witness students eagerly making changes in their writing; thus, the revision process is continued (see chapter 4 for minilesson on revision).

We facilitate students' familiarization with unknown words by making thesauruses and dictionaries available on their desks. To alleviate any uncertainty that may arise when seemingly mismatched words are selected, we model a prewriting technique that attacks each word separately. The teacher creates a cluster for each word, and then the writer considers both lists of ideas and images to use in creating a poem.

Our classroom experiences with mystery slips show that even the most reluctant writers are motivated to write because they have hundreds of possibilities available from which to select words. Occasionally, students plagued by writer's block request to draw from the mystery slips during other poetry writing activities.

ACTIVITY 7   Shake Up a Word

Objectives
• To compose poetry that extends a writer's perceptions of particular words
• To compose poetry that reflects personal experiences and connections

Procedure
This activity began with our reading of *A Celebration of Bees: Helping Children Write Poetry* (Esbensen, 1995). The teacher selects a word and leads the class in a brainstorm about the word. First, students put their heads down and close their eyes while the teacher asks the brainstorming questions. Next, as the teacher repeats the questions, students record their thoughts. Then, in either small groups or as a whole class, students share their ideas. The teacher invites students to borrow strong words and ideas from their classmates.

Once this sharing is completed, students draft their poems. Next, conferencing begins again, with Graves's (1992) focus questions on display (see chapter 4, page 51). Through practice, students become adept at responding to one another's poetry; moreover, they internalize how to respond productively.

This shake-up-a-word process can be repeated for as many words as the teacher believes valuable. We begin with the word *fire*, as Esbensen (1995) demonstrates with the following directives:

• What is the feeling of fire?

• What are other words besides hot?

• What words mean fire?

• Do any flowers make you think of fire?

• Do any tastes remind you of fire?

• What smells like fire?

• What animal moves like a flame?

• What jewels are like fire?

• Picture fire. What is burning? How does it look?

• Can you hear the fire?

• What are the sound words for fire?

• What color is fire?

• Write down any fiery scenes you can see in your mind.

• What is the opposite of fire? (p. 20)

Teachers can modify and elaborate on the questions using other words. In our classrooms, we focus on the five senses, asking questions that we believe will encourage students to think about the word differently. For example, when shaking up "fire," students can be inspired to write about a camping trip, the sun, or a flame.

In the following poem, the student creates a picture of flames for readers using metaphors such as "blazing tail of a fox" and "endless dance." Readers immediately see the movement of fire through the personification of "dancing flames." The author's use of strong words, such as "endless seared flames" and "dissolving teeth and tongue," show the influence of brainstorming before drafting. The brainstorming serves as a means to extend students' thinking about the word.

Dancing Flames

flickering
flame
against my face
sizzling
scorch
blazing tail of a fox
dissolving
teeth and tongue
endless seared flames
flowing like lava
crashing on me
like waves
they flicker
and dance
hot
sparks tear my eyes
endless
dance
flickering
flames

—JENNIE, AGE 12

The questions posed by the teacher influence another student to include her own questions in the following poem. The responses to these questions focus on the sense of touch: "cold, blistery winter" and "little children with cold hands and feet." To introduce the sense of sight, the student uses metaphors such as "bright red of a cardinal," "mellow yellow of the sun," and "warm orange of an orange."

Fire

What wants it?
Cold, blistery winter wants it
Who wants it?
Little children with cold hands and feet want it
Fire
Bright red of a cardinal
Mellow yellow of the sun
Warm orange of an orange

Tongues licking up into the air
That's fire

—MARY, AGE 11

Another student uses onomatopoeia in the following poem to illustrate the qualities of fire and its opposite—ice.

Opposites

Fire
Snap! Crackle! Pop!
Burning.
Ice
Ting! Crack! Sizzle!
Freezing.

—JERRY, AGE 11

Another word we shake up is *season*. Students think and write about various topics including memories, objects, and sports.

Mr. and Mrs. Winter

Mr. and Mrs. Winter
Do you make the snow?
You know I love snow.
So why don't you bring some?
Sprinkle it on my nose.
Mr. and Mrs. Winter
There's but one thing I don't like
It's that pesky dog of yours
He really likes to bite
My nose
And my toes
And my fingers and my cheeks

So Mr. and Mrs. Winter
If that's not too much trouble
Keep that Frosty locked up inside
Away from me and my mother!

—MALIA, AGE 11

Leaves

Snap Crackle Pop
The sound just never stops
Orange Yellow Red and Green
Leaves are anything but clean
Prickly Pokey Pointy Spots
That...
Snap Crackle Pop
Those leaves just never stop

—Emma, age 11

The Four Seasons

Winter with snowballs, Smack!
Spring with baseball, Whack!
Summer with swimming, Splash!
Fall with football, Hike!

I hate them all...
Psyche!

—Bobby, age 11

When the word *storm* becomes the focus of our questions, it, too, generates various types of poems and topics associated with it.

Storm

The sharp, jagged lightning bolts
cut through the sky like a knife
through warm butter
The elephant gray sky looks you in the eye
The roaring wind takes charge
the bam of thunder shouts out at you
Telephone posts drop like
hollow sticks and look as light as feathers
The sound is an angry elephant
Trash cans zip through the streets
Bullets of rain pound on the houses with no conscience

—Zac, age 12

War in the Sky

Howling like a lonely dog
Thunder booms
Zeus throws bolts of lightning
Fresh rainfall air
Lawn chairs blown over
Flying cows
Satin rainbow
Snap, crackle, pop
Burnt marshmallows
Crack of a whip
War in the sky

—WILL, AGE 12

Chills and Thrills

The chills and thrills
Of a
Tornado storm
Inviting you to play
It whistles to you
Like a train
As a jagged yellow bolt
Splits the sky
Fear
Comes upon you
As the sky changes
From light to
Dark
Sirens
In and out of your head
Then the
Fresh spring flowers
Pop-up like
A shooting rubber band
The storm has passed.

—SARAH, AGE 12

Rain

Hey, Mr. Rain,
I'm in a drought,
Please pour rain all out,
I'd like to get soaked, and wet,
To be able to jump all about,
I love the sound of drip drop,
Don't forget I'm in a drought,
I need you desperately
I need more of you,
To live, to play,
Please, Mr. Rain, pour on me,
I will beg and plead,
Please, Mr. Rain, please pour on me.

—KEITH, AGE 11

Wrapping Up

One benefit of this activity is that students frequently access the Poet's Toolbox (see Appendix A) while composing, conferencing, and revising. Another benefit is that students extend their perceptions of words beyond the commonplace, and their personal connections and experiences visibly enrich the writing. Other words that have inspired our students to write poems include *city*, *night*, *ocean*, and *morning*. Teachers and students can find unlimited possibilities from their own environments.

Objectives
• To compose poetry
• To make students cognizant of the power of words

Procedure
In the prior activities, students have considered words in novel ways. This activity augments their repertoire of writing ideas with their own and others' words in a concrete way. We created this activity after reading *Awakening the Heart* (Heard, 1999).

First, in the classroom setting, the teacher asks students to brainstorm a list of specific, everyday words that relate to their lives—what they know, see, hear, smell, taste, and feel. This brainstorming is done as a whole class, and a variety of words emerge as students write their ideas on pink index cards. After a few minutes, the teacher collects the index cards. Next, the teacher has the class move outside—to the football field, playground, or tennis court—and repeat the brainstorm of everyday words, inspired by the outdoor sights and sounds. Students write these words on green index cards that the teacher also collects. The process is repeated using white index cards, with the focus of the brainstorm on a room in the students' homes.

The teacher shuffles the pink, green, and white index cards, lays them on the ground, and then directs students to choose 10 to 15 cards. First, students arrange the word cards as a poem. They read the words aloud, listening to the sounds of the words, and then they arrange the words in lines of poetry. While drafting the lines of poetry, students may add words and images as they see fit. This array of words serves as a prewriting for poetry.

As words such as *clouds, leaves, laughter, sun,* and *hill* appear on index cards, students are inspired to make connections between words relating to their everyday environments and their own life experiences. For example, in the prewriting of the following poems, one student connects the school environment to a beach, and another student remembers riding a snowboard and composes images of the experience.

Will I Ever Be Back?

Will I ever be back
To this place that I love?
Will I ever be back
On the warm, bronze, soft sand that is peppered with
    footprints?
Will I ever be back
To feel the clear, crystal water tickling my feet?

Will I ever be back
To know the warm sun on my back?
Will I ever be back
And hear the calming lapping of the water?
Will I ever be back
To hear waves as they reach up to tease the shore
Or the rustling of the palm trees' leaves?
Will I ever be back
To hear the children's laughter?
Will I ever be back
To feel the peacefulness, calmness, and welcome that I felt
    before?
Will I ever be back?
I wonder...
Will I ever be back?

—ANDREA, AGE 12

Amazing Ride

Teeth-chattering wind,
Propelling the snowboard,
Down a white, fluffy hill.
Suddenly,
Hit jagged snow,
Hurl into the air,
Look down,
Realize you're flying.
Flying through the cotton ball clouds.
Now the air is refreshing,
Like cool lemonade,
On a scorching summer day.

—TIM, AGE 12

Wrapping Up

One of the goals of poetry workshop is to position students as writers for an audience. This activity makes students aware of how to capture that audience through the power of words while conveying a message to readers and igniting pictures in their minds.

ACTIVITY 9   Imagery

Objectives
• To compose poetry with images that appeal to all five senses
• To use literary devices to strengthen imagery

Procedure
As students gain confidence in themselves as poets, ideas for poems come to them more easily. This activity reinforces the use of imagery to strengthen poetry writing, conveying pictures to readers who can more readily transact with the text. To begin this activity, the teacher displays the poem "The Space" by Gary Soto (see page 42).

Using a graphic organizer for imagery (see Appendix C), students analyze the poem for its use of imagery, citing words and phrases that create pictures by appealing to the five senses. Using the organizer stretches students' thinking about a topic beyond an observer's first impressions to the nuances that may be overlooked. A whole-class discussion follows that highlights how the poet creates pictures for the reader. Students cite particular lines and phrases that show simile, personification, and other figures of speech. Students employ the same graphic organizer to generate a list of words and phrases that describe a busy setting of their choice.

The effectiveness of this activity increases if students go to their busy setting. If possible, the whole class may move outdoors so students can use their natural surroundings as the basis of their brainstorming. On a January morning after a light snowfall, Teresa took her students to the front steps of the school. Flurries continued to fall as students filled their graphic organizers with words and phrases that appealed to their senses. The resulting poems that follow show the effectiveness of the students' use of imagery.

In the first poem, the student creates powerful images, extending his thinking and observations beyond his initial visual impressions. The use of the metaphor "an army of snowflakes" conveys the movement and density of snowflakes—"Invading and covering everything." The student's use of onomatopoeia—"crunch" and "crack"—appeals to the sense of hearing; the use of simile—"your own breath like steam"—appeals to the sense of touch, illustrating cold.

A Winter Day
A winter day
In the early morning
The sound of shovelers
Shoveling

The Space

West of town,
Near Hermosa's well,
I sleep sometimes—
In a hammock, of course—
Among avocado trees,
Cane, spider-grass,
The hatchet-faced chula,
The banana's umbrella
Of leaves.
It is here
In the spiny brush
Where cocks gabble.
Where the javelina
Lies on its side
Like an overturned high-heel.
I say it is enough
To be where the smells
Of creatures
Braid like rope
And to know if
The grasses' rustle
is only
A lizard passing.
It is enough, brother,
Listening to a bird coo
A leash of parables
Keeping an eye
On the moon.
The space between cork trees
When the sun first appears.

— GARY SOTO

From Soto, G. (1995). New and Selected Poems. *Used with permission of Chronicle Books.*

An army of snowflakes
Falling
Invading and covering everything
Snow falling off trees and on your head
Looking like dandruff in your hair
Slushing from cars on the street
Slish, Slash
Crunching of snow as you walk
Crunch
Cracking of ice as you walk
Crack
Sight of your own breath
Like steam
As snow silently falls
Old Man Winter is good at his job

—NATHAN, AGE 11

Using the graphic organizer compelled the writer of the following poem to include myriad sights, describing them with figurative language. The student compares the snow "covering our school" to a white sheet and personifies snow "hiding" from the sun that is "peeking." The details he includes—"wet street," "crisp layer of bitterness in the air," and "harmless shoveler scraping"—create images in readers' minds.

The School's Snow

A white sheet
is covering our school
and is hiding from
the peeking sun
a harmless shoveler
is scraping away
at the ground
and the cars
are swishing
down the wet street
there is a crisp
layer of bitterness
in the air
it makes the air
heavy
the last crystals
of the day
fall
on my head
as I wait
for the next
winter's night storm

—SHANE, AGE 11

In the following two poems, students demonstrate the power of the graphic organizer to stretch their own thinking of a busy place during a snowfall—yielding different results, each creating a rich collection of images for readers.

Forest of White Dreams

A nice quiet
place
The forest of white
dreams
with miles of white
arched trees
a peaceful quiet place
the sleek smooth
soft, freshly
fallen snow
is like silk
running through
your fingers,
the forest of
overturned snow cones
is to the north
and the palace
of white dreams is
to the south
but best of all
the forest of white dreams
is here with me

—OWEN, AGE 11

Snow Fell, Snow Falls

The sky sees tall trees
dressed in snow,
some wearing leaves
some wearing no

The ground sees
glowing snow
falling snow
smooth snow
soft snow, on the go

Snow that could fill seas
Strong and silent trees
footprints like white spice
in the snow and growing ice
houses of old
immune to cold

Weighing down trees
falling down
beautiful snow
no one can frown

The last of the squirrels
hunting for the last of the nuts
risking, edging toward humans
moving in struts
the first flake falls
The first flake fell

the first flake lands
and that is all

—Joshua, age 11

Wrapping Up

The powerful results in the previous poems make it clear that the graphic organizer is the conduit for making students acutely conscious of the five senses and moves them to stretch their thinking when writing about a topic. This brainstorming activity generates multiple choices and images for students to access as they compose. It is important for teachers to emphasize to students that all the details produced in the brainstorm are not required to appear in the poem.

ACTIVITY 10   Me Poem

Objective
• To communicate a description of oneself through poetry writing

Procedure
Adolescents search for meaning, struggling to discover who they are and where they are going in life. Writing about self is a subject in which middle school students become easily invested. This workshop begins with a brainstorming activity focusing each student on him- or herself.

   The teacher explains to the students that it is easy to describe the physical aspects of a person, but it is not as easy to convey what is in a person's heart. The teacher explains that the me poem will communicate to readers a personal description—how the poet sees him- or herself. The teacher shares a sample of his or her me poem, giving students a glimpse of the teacher as a writer, an equal participant, and facilitator of poetry workshop.

Butterfly
Me
Talk, talk, talk
Knit, knit, knit
Read & write, read & write
Talk, knit, read & write
Butterfly
Work out, work out, work out
Beach, beach, beach
Friend & husband, friend & husband
Work out, beach, friend & husband
Sisters, brother, nephews, nieces
Butterfly
I'm a butterfly
That's me!

—Teresa Morretta

   Then, the teacher asks students questions that focus on various traits. The teacher asks the following probing questions while students close their eyes:

   • What do you see when you look in the mirror?

   • How tall are you?

- What animal are you like? How?
- Is there a flower that reminds you of yourself? How?
- What color describes your personality? Why?
- What makes you a good friend?
- What are three words that describe you?
- What sports do you play or like?

Next, the teacher repeats the questions and students brainstorm answers, an activity that serves as prewriting. Students draft poems and then conference about them in small groups, sharing responses and making suggestions. Whole-class conferencing follows with students volunteering to read aloud their poems.

Me

I see myself,
My short brown hair,
My eyes so sharp,
My height average,
I see myself,
A cunning fox,
I move so quick,
And never stop
My shirt is yellow,
So radiant and bright,
If you took an x-ray,
Then you would see,
I'm goofy, helpful, and trustworthy
And at my feet a soccer ball
To kick and score
And shout
Shout
Shout
So this is me
As you can see
Don't mix me up
I'm me

—BRIAN, AGE 11

Me

I am me
Dark brown hair
Dark brown eyes
I am me
No
One
Else

—AMANDA, AGE 11

Me

Brown hair, brown eyes, caring and funny
How great it is to be me!
Softball, baseball, field hockey
How great it is to be me!
Friendly, active, trustworthy
How great it is to be me!
Talking, talking, talking
How great it is to be me!

—CHELSEY, AGE 11

Me

As I look into the mirror I see
A familiar face staring back at me.
Who is that?
Eyes the color of the drifting sea.
Who is that?
Hair of the color of the bark on a tree.
Who is that?
Skin the color of sand as it slips through your fingertips.
Who is that?
Oops, sorry.
That person is me!

—ELIZABETH, AGE 11

Wrapping Up

Because we envision poetry writing as an opportunity for students to make sense of themselves, the world, and texts, The "me poem" activity enables them to communicate personal meaning of all three. The me poem provides students with an opportunity to make meaning of themselves, offering a forum to communicate their self-image during a pivotal time in their development.

This activity also can be extended to have students write about important people in their lives—a "you poem." Students are motivated to write about people in their lives who incite emotions such as fear, joy, sadness, grief, and excitement. Another variation is to have students answer the me poem questions in the role of a character from text. This response to literature requires students to think as the character, thus evoking literary analysis.

Using the activities in this chapter, students convey personal meaning through poetry writing. The activities facilitate student thinking about ideas—the basis for their creative, powerful communication. Student writers, employing their individual writing styles, expand their experiences with words to create images for readers. The resulting poems are as diverse as the students themselves.

Now that students have amassed a repertoire of their own poems, chapter 4 addresses the next step. Just as professional writers make revisions and prepare their pieces for publication, students in poetry workshop approach their writing in a similar way.

CHAPTER 4

Taking the Next Steps With Poetry Writing

Since poetry workshop began, students have known the answer to the question, What's next after drafting? Students are aware that conferencing, revision, and publication are also key components of the writing process. Most writers compose with these components in mind. Throughout the school year, our students are positioned as writers for an audience, and they understand that they write for readers, sharing through small-group and whole-class conferences and revising their writing as they consider classmates' and teacher's feedback. In poetry workshop, students listen carefully and make meaningful revisions because publication is a natural goal.

Another key component of poetry workshop is assessment. Teachers, who are accountable for student learning, must observe student poets and gauge their growth. We have included a formal assessment in this chapter to obtain concrete evidence of students' development as writers.

Conferencing

Conferencing is conversation that leads to revision. Students listen and respond to another's writing by giving constructive feedback. Because of their participation in literature circle discussions, students listen and respond to others' opinions and evaluations about texts, making them comfortable with the conversational aspect of conferencing. Conferencing is the first step in the process of revision—looking at writing with a critical eye and making changes. For middle school writers, conferencing provides specific, tangible focus points that they can consider, which will help to improve both themselves as writers and their writing.

Conversations about their poems prompt students to take a second look at their pieces. Students make choices about their use of language and think critically about how and what they are communicating to readers, elucidating that revision plays a significant role in written communication. Once students have a work in progress, they volunteer to share aloud their poems in small groups. The teacher directs students to respond critically to the poem, guided by the following questions from Graves (1992):

- What struck you about the poem?
- Did any particular words create interesting pictures? What do you see in these pictures?
- Were there any words you especially liked? Why?
- What did you wonder about?
- What do you suppose the poet was thinking when he or she wrote the poem? What makes you think so? (p. 16)

Once students begin to respond to one another's writing, the student writer takes notes on the suggestions made by peers. The conversations among students are meaningful exchanges that propel them into the revision process.

Next, students volunteer to read aloud their poems to the whole class, following the same procedure as above. Although these questions may appear to produce canned responses, what actually emerge are real conversations among students with the writer. As they conference, students extend their responses to include suggestions for the writer based on their own experiences as poets. They discuss the poem with the student poet—not with the teacher. Although as a writer the teacher is an equal participant in the writing community, the teacher is not an expert, but is a facilitator; thus, the teacher's poems are read and discussed in the same way as students' poetry.

Revision

Writers revise at all stages of the writing process to make their meaning clear to readers. Although revision occurs informally during the activities in the preceding chapters, the activity offered in this section makes writers cognizant of its power. This activity, with its focus on poetry writing, offers students concrete ways to reconsider their works. Students see the effects of revision through the discussions and the application of the lessons to their own writing.

Mary Lynn Ellis, coauthor of *With a Poet's Eye* (McVeigh-Schultz & Ellis, 1997), led a workshop on revision in Teresa's classroom titled "How to Polish a Poem Until

It Shines," and her following points proved to be effective in teaching poetry revision to middle school writers.

1. Decide where you want the poem to take a breath. At the end of each line and each stanza is a breath.
2. Delete all unnecessary words.
3. Add details to get the poem to come alive. Be specific—don't say *animal* when you mean *armadillo*.
4. Make sure every word is right. Be very precise.
5. Find the best first line.
6. Find the best last line.
7. Discover a strong title, phrase, or poem subject.

Using "Mother to Son" by Langston Hughes, begin the session with a teacher-led discussion on the seven points listed above. The following analysis of the poem serves as a conduit for students to understand why Ellis's suggestions are a valuable script for teachers.

The first time the teacher reads the poem aloud, the students' goal is to hear and understand its message. Next, a copy of the poem is displayed and the teacher rereads the poem, leading minilessons on revision—polishing a poem. The teacher emphasizes the importance of line breaks—where the reader takes a breath.

In "Mother to Son," the first line directly addresses the speaker's son; the use of the colon at the end of the first line marks a deep breath for the reader and imitates the style of a letter. In the second line, the poet introduces a metaphor for the mother's life—"no crystal stair." The poet goes on to delineate four examples of how the mother's life is "no crystal stair." The placement of these descriptions on four separate lines creates a strong image because the reader is made to take a breath and observe, pausing to visualize "tacks," "splinters," "boards torn up," and "no carpet on the floor." After this description of her life, the poet places "bare" punctuated with a period on a separate line, forcing the reader to stop and recognize the seriousness of the struggle that the mother is communicating to her son. Following these examples, the teacher can continue to investigate the poet's arrangement of lines throughout the poem.

The teacher now focuses the discussion on Hughes's use of specific details, making the poem come alive. Hughes uses "landin's" and "corners" to extend the metaphor. These details not only create images for the reader but also give the connotations deeper meaning. The use of "landin's" suggests that the speaker has come

Mother to Son

Well, son, I'll tell you:
Life for me ain't been no crystal stair.
It's had tacks in it,
And splinters,
And boards torn up,
And places with no carpet on the floor—
Bare.
But all the time
I'se been a-climbin' on,
And reachin' landin's,
And turnin' corners,
And sometimes goin' in the dark
Where there ain't been no light.
So, boy, don't you turn back.
Don't you set down on the steps
'Cause you finds it kinder hard.
Don't you fall now—
For I'se still goin', honey,
I'se still climbin',
And life for me ain't been no crystal stair.

—LANGSTON HUGHES

From The Collected Poems of Langston Hughes, copyright © 1994 by the Estate of Languston Hughes. Used with permission of Alfred A Knopf, Random House, Inc.

far to reach her present state in life. The use of "corners" points to the conflicts she faced as she struggled to reach the present.

Next, the teacher discusses Hughes's use of words. The poet employs the "right words"—dialect that reflects the culture of the speaker of the poem. The word choices "son," "boy," and "honey" depict the relationship between the mother and her son. The poet uses "goin' in the dark" and "where there ain't been no light" to stress that there have been bleak times in the mother's journey through life. These examples illustrate to students that precise language makes a poem more powerful.

A discussion follows about the effectiveness of the first and last lines of the poem. The first line establishes the speaker's purpose and shows the relationship between the speaker and her son. The last line sustains the image of her life as "no crystal stair." The last line is a full circle, repeating the metaphor, and emphasizes the mother's message to her son—keep trying despite obstacles of life.

Students are now ready to polish their poems, applying what they have learned from this poem's example. Each student selects one poem to revise, and students work in pairs using the points from "How to Polish a Poem Until It Shines" to guide them. The first student reads aloud his or her poem to a peer. Together, the pair discusses the student writer's arrangement of lines, use of particular words and punctuation, choice of details, and reasons for first and last lines. Then the poet can decide to make changes to strengthen the poem. The pair repeats this process for the other student's poem. Next, students change partners. Each student in the pair shares the first draft and revised draft of his or her poem. A discussion of the changes follows. The teacher circulates around the classroom, adding to the pairs' conversations. Then, the teacher asks for volunteers to explain their revisions to the whole class. Afterward, in anticipation of the poetry anthology that the class will publish, students work individually to revise the poems that they plan to include. Then, students conference with one another, discussing their revisions. This activity demonstrates to students that revision is a crucial step in the writing process. The following examples illustrate the effectiveness of students' revisions.

Figure 2 demonstrates a student's revision of his personal response to "I, Too" by Langston Hughes (see Appendix D). The student begins the revision process by deciding how to arrange the words in particular lines. In a few instances, he deletes unnecessary words that he realizes impede the poem's rhythm. The sentences are transformed into lines of poetry in which line breaks signal a pause to the reader. Changes in meaning are evident when students compare initial drafts and published poems. The student also gives thoughtful consideration to the poem's title, changing "He Sings America" to "Sing America." He also makes editing changes for spelling, subject-verb agreement, and capitalization.

FIGURE 2
Student Revision Process

Sing America

He isn't allowed to eat
With his company
He looks at the positive side
And eats well
He grows strong

He has faith
He stands up for himself
He sits at the table
Tomorrow no one will stop him

He gets dressed up
And impresses them all

He is American
He loves this country

—JOE, AGE 11

Figure 3 (see page 56) shows the revision of the student poem "The Chaotic Lunchroom." While revising the draft of the poem, the student changes line 6, "They tease and won't stop," to "They scream and tease and never stop." The new line is a conscious decision to use the "magic 3"—a literary device taught in our language arts classes. In magic 3, a writer organizes words, phrases, or sentences in a series of three, thereby creating rhythm for the writing. By removing "worst" from line 3, the student strengthens his message. When asked why he removed the descriptor, he explained that the teacher had this nightmare every night, and "worst" meant that the teacher had other nightmares. The student also edits for spelling.

FIGURE 3
Student Revision Process

The Chaotic Lunchroom

Chit, Chat,

Food Fight,

The teacher's nightmare,

A chaotic lunchroom,

Where everyone's wild,

They scream and tease and
 never stop,

Food in the air,

Everyone stares,

It hits a kid,

Who falls to the ground,

Mashed potatoes on the ground,

Whipped cream pies on people's faces,

SPLAT!

Uh-oh, it hit the principal!

—KEITH, AGE 11

Tim's revision of "Amazing Ride" (see Figure 4) shows that he is cognizant that word choice makes a difference in the message he communicates to the reader. Lines 1 and 2 of his draft read "The teeth-chattering wind/blows as you snowboard." In lines 1 and 2 of the published poem, the wind is no longer merely the setting of a snowboard ride. "Teeth-chattering wind/Propelling the snowboard" shows that now the wind is moving the snowboard and carrying the speaker in the poem down the hill. The student's strong word choices—"propelling" and "hurl"—create more vivid images for readers. The student writer recognizes the need to make line breaks in order to guide readers in the reading of his poem.

FIGURE 4
Student Revision Process

Amazing Ride

Teeth-chattering wind,
Propelling the snowboard,
Down a white, fluffy hill.
Suddenly,
Hit jagged snow,
Hurl into the air,
Look down,
Realize you're flying,
Flying through the cotton ball
    clouds.
Now the air is refreshing,
Like cool lemonade,
On a scorching summer day.

—TIM, AGE 12

SOUND POEM

The teeth-chattering wind,
blows as you Propelling the snowboard,
down a white, fluffy hill.
Suddenly you hit jagged snow,
and go hurling into the air,
look down realize your flying,
flying through the cotton ball clouds.
Now the air is refreshing,
like a cool lemonade,
on a scorching summer day.

Publication

In our classrooms, students are writers for readers, cognizant that they write for many audiences—themselves, teachers, parents, the school community, and the public at large. Throughout the school year, the recursive writing process is emphasized—prewriting, drafting, conferencing, revising, conferencing, editing, and publishing. Students experience writing as time-consuming and difficult work; moreover, they discern that writing improves only by conferencing and thoughtful revision.

Because publishing is a natural, meaningful, and expected goal for writers, students are offered the following opportunities for publishing their poetry: professional publishing, a class anthology, and a poetry book. Two valuable resources that provide students with professional publishing opportunities are *Writer's Market* (Brogan & Brewer, 2002) and *A Young Writer's Guide to Getting Published* (Henderson, 2001). (See Appendix E for a list of professional publishing opportunities.)

For the class anthology, each student selects five poems written during poetry workshop. Students prepare their poems for submission by typing the poems and including clip art or illustrations. Each student in the class receives a copy of the anthology.

For the poetry book, each student selects 8 to 10 poems written during poetry workshop. The students prepare the poems in the same way as for the class anthology. Each book is displayed in the classroom for students to read. (See Appendix F for a rubric for this assignment.)

Assessment

Publication of student poems is a celebration and a concrete sign to students and teachers of the learning that transpires in poetry workshop. Although throughout poetry workshop teachers informally assess students' work, local school districts and state departments of education mandate formal assessments; therefore, we developed the following two assessments to document student learning.

Analytical Assessment

After students complete poetry workshop, the class discusses how a poem can be assessed fairly. In small groups, students consider what constitutes a "good" poem, discussing what poets do to engage readers. Students record their responses, mindful of the five domains of writing (focus, organization, content, style, and conventions) and how writers use strong words and literary devices.

Next, in a whole-class discussion, students share their ideas. The students and teacher choose the most important criteria from the class list of ideas. Students may decide that poets should engage readers (style and content), use language clearly (focus and organization), and use punctuation purposefully (conventions) to create a good poem. Then, the teacher discusses past rubrics, connecting to what the students have learned about writing. The class decides how the determined criteria relate to the five domains of effective writing.

The teacher shares the completed rubric, which the class uses to evaluate sample poems. The teacher presents several poems for evaluation; some of the poems engage readers more effectively than others do. Each student chooses one of his or her poems to assess, keeping in mind the class-generated rubric the teacher uses (see Figure 5). This process makes students aware that they are writers for readers; moreover, they synthesize their learning about writing. This practice readies students to reflect on their own writing.

Holistic Assessment

We created a formal assessment as a take-home test (see Appendix G) that asks students to think critically about the poetry-writing process, making them accountable

FIGURE 5
Rubric for a Good Poem

A "good" poem engages the reader by creating images.	Advanced—4	Proficient—3	Basic—2	Below Basic—1
Style: Strong word choice, sensory images, literary devices	The writer uses many strong word choices, sensory images, or literary devices.	The writer uses some strong word choices, sensory images, or literary devices.	The writer uses few strong word choices, sensory images, or literary devices.	The writer does not develop ideas, lacking strong word choices, sensory images, or literary devices.
Content: Idea developed	The writer develops idea in a sophisticated way.	The writer develops an idea.	The writer attempts to develop an idea.	No idea developed.
Focus and organization: Clear use of language	The writer's poem has a clear focus.	The writer's poem has an apparent focus.	The writer's poem has a vague focus.	The writer's poem lacks focus.
	The writer arranges words and lines to convey meaning in a sophisticated way.	The writer arranges words and lines to convey meaning.	The writer's arrangement of words and lines does not effectively convey meaning to readers.	The writer's arrangement of words and lines confuses readers.
Conventions: Purposeful use of punctuation	Punctuation enhances writer's poem.	Writer chooses punctuation to convey meaning.	Writer shows some use of punctuation to convey meaning.	Punctuation is random—chosen without thought to the meaning conveyed.

for their learning. Students support their opinions, showing critical thinking; discuss figurative language (the techniques writers use to engage readers); and communicate how revision has affected their writing. By citing specific examples from their poems, students elucidate that poetry workshop has influenced them as writers (see Figures 6a, 6b, and 6c). These student assessments show that poetry workshop has made a difference in students' understanding of themselves as writers.

FIGURE 6A
A Page From Conor's Student Assessment

Grade yourself after each essay 15/16 *nice!*

Name *Conor* 6-M   Due Date *Mon Feb 3*

94

Poetry Assessment – Take Home Assignment

Directions:
- Answer in complete sentences, using your **daily writing journal** with the poetry drafts.
- You will need to use **stickees** to place in your journal to mark the poems you are discussing; **label** the stickees with the test question number.
- You will need a **highlighter** to highlight the lines you are discussing in your poem.

1. Did your feeling about poetry reading and poetry writing change in any way after you completed Poetry Workshop? If yes, explain how it has changed. If no, explain why you believe it did not. Be **thorough**—support your explanation.

I think that poetry workshop definately helped me because I can write much better poems then I would be able to before. I think the activitys really helped me, like when we listened to music and then wrote poems describing it. That helped alot because it helped me learn how to describe different sound even without the words. Another good activity that helped me was when we picked and adjective and a verb out of a box and wrote a poem using that as the title. I think that a good poem that I wrote using that was about a nonchalant classroom. Since we had an adjective and a verb so you really have to describe the classroom and use other words that mean nonchalant to describe the classroom. Another good activity that helped me was called the Before and After. In this we pick something and then write what its like before you use it, while you're using it and then after you've used it. I did a snowboard and described how it gets chipped and scratched after you use it. So overall, I think poetry workshop did a great job making me a better poet.

Reading, Writing, Speaking, & Listening Standards					
1.1 Read independently.					
1.3 Read, analyze, and interpret literature.					
1.4 Write in various modes.					
1.5 Produce writing of high quality.					
1.7 Understand the characteristic and functions of the English language.					

4 (3.5)	3	2	1	0
Accurate, **specific** explanation of thinking, offering **thorough** support of opinion.	**General** explanation of thinking, offering **some** support of opinion.	Inaccurate, **vague**, or incomplete explanation that **lacks support** of opinion.	Somewhat related to the question, but **does not answer** the specific question.	Illegible or no answer

FIGURE 6B
A Page From Margo's Student Assessment

2. In your daily writing journal, find a poem that contains **figurative language**.
   - Place a stickee on the page where the poem is and write #2.
   - Highlight the line in the poem that contains the example.
   - In the space below, identify what the device is (for example: simile, personification, etc.) and explain **how** it made your poem stronger.

✓ doesn't matter which e

The figurative language that is used in my poem (What I love) is a simile. It made my poem stronger, because It gives you a great Image of how happy I am, because little kids always are happy on their birthdays. That is how the figurative language, simile, made my poem a lot stronger. Also, It isn't a metaphore because I use the word Like, and metaphores don't use like or as.

4	3	2	1	0
Accurate, **specific** explanation of thinking, offering **thorough** support of opinion; shows true understanding of figurative language.	**General** explanation of thinking, offering **some** support of opinion; shows general understanding of figurative language.	Inaccurate, **vague**, or incomplete explanation that **lacks support** of opinion; shows limited understanding of figurative language.	Somewhat related to the question, but **does not answer** the specific question; shows a lack of understanding of figurative language.	Illegible or no answer

— same thing as 3

3. Find **another** poem that contains **figurative language**.
   - Place a stickee on the page where the poem is and write #3.
   - Highlight the line in the poem that contains the example.
   - In the space below, identify what the device is (for example: simile, personification, etc.) and explain **how** it made your poem stronger.

The figurative language that I used in my snow poem was onomatopeia. The onomatopeia helped to make my poem stronger. The onomatopeia (sound word) I used was "swoosh", and it was describing the sound of the cars passing in the snow When I hear the word swoosh, I can automaticly hear a car passing in the rain, and that is the sound I want the reader to hear when they read my poem.

4	3	2	1	0
Accurate, **specific** explanation of thinking, offering **thorough** support of opinion; shows true understanding of figurative language.	**General** explanation of thinking, offering **some** support of opinion; shows general understanding of figurative language.	Inaccurate, **vague**, or incomplete explanation that **lacks support** of opinion; shows limited understanding of figurative language.	Somewhat related to the question, but **does not answer** the specific question; shows a lack of understanding of figurative language.	Illegible or no answer

FIGURE 6C
A Page From Joe's Student Assessment

4. Revision of poetry writing is important to the writer and reader of poetry. In your daily writing journal, find a poem that shows **revision**.
- Place a stickee on the page where the poem is, and draw a star to mark the poem.
- In the space below, **explain** the revisions you made and why you made them. Discuss **how** it made your poem stronger.
- Be **thorough**—support your explanation.

I made revisions to my poem, Seasons. I think these revisions made my poem much stronger. In my poem one of the revisions I made was to cross out unnesesary words like they is, but, it, it's, etc. The reason I take out these words is because it makes my poem stronger. It makes it stronger because when you cross out those words it sounds more like poetry because that is how a lot of poetry is written. I just think taking out these words makes my poem much better.

Another revision I use is putting part of a line on a different line. I think this makes my poem stronger because somtimes I want the reader to stop reading in between a line so I move the part where I want them to pause on a seperate line. This is a very important revision for me, and it works.

I think revising a poem is one of the most important parts of poetry because with out it most of my poems wouldn't be strong.

4	3	2	1	0
Accurate, **specific** explanation of thinking, offering **thorough** support of opinion; shows true understanding of revision.	**General** explanation of thinking, offering **some** support of opinion; shows general understanding of revision.	Inaccurate, **vague**, or incomplete explanation that **lacks support** of opinion; shows limited understanding of revision.	Somewhat related to the question, but **does not answer** the specific question; shows a lack of understanding of revision.	Illegible or no answer

In poetry workshop, the reading and writing of poetry are transactions that honor the poet, the poem, and the reader. With an understanding of—and the experiences as—both readers and writers of poetry, students connect, evaluate, and reflect on text, self, and world. In chapter 5, we demonstrate how poetry writing can be used to communicate student learning across the curriculum and as responses to reading. We include objectives, discussion, and student examples to illustrate how poetry writing is valuable as an alternative assessment.

CHAPTER 5

Responding as Poets Outside of Poetry Workshop

After students experience poetry workshop, they are comfortable with and knowledgeable about poetry writing. Now, the teacher may use poetry writing as a response to learning and texts across the curriculum, and students can integrate their understanding of poetry writing with their learning outside of poetry workshop.

The various poetry-writing activities in this chapter are alternatives to traditional responses to texts such as essays, tests, book reports, and journals. The accompanying student examples illuminate their understanding of particular topics in many curricular areas.

Objectives
- To provide students with experiences in which they critically read and discuss a poet's writing
- To give students opportunities to explore and enjoy poets' works, reading poetry as writers

Procedure

The poet study truly positions students as readers who write and writers who read. During poetry workshop, students learn and practice what poets do to communicate meaning—literary devices and revision techniques. During the poet study, students, cognizant of the genre's nuances, critically read and discuss poetry as writers who have composed poetry.

Literature circles are a common practice in our classrooms, so the structure of the poet study is one that our students find familiar. To form literature circles, the teacher uses the jigsaw method—a type of cooperative learning group where each student is assigned both a home group and an expert group. Students first meet in their home groups, where each member selects a poet about whom he or she will become an expert. The home groups disperse and students convene in expert groups—reading the same collection of poems by the same poet. Expert groups can be formed for the following suggested classic and contemporary poets and texts:

- *Poetry for Young People: Emily Dickinson*
- *Poetry for Young People: Robert Frost*
- *Poetry for Young People: Edgar Allen Poe*
- *The Dream Keeper and Other Poems* by Langston Hughes
- *Everywhere Faces Everywhere: Poems* by James Berry
- *Joyful Noise: Poems for Two Voices* by Paul Fleischman
- *Ordinary Things: Poems From a Walk in Early Spring* by Ralph Fletcher

Meeting in expert groups, students read the poems aloud. Each student takes notes while reading and during any discussion of the poems using sticky notes that can be affixed to the page. The teacher displays guiding questions to focus students' notes and discussion:

- What poems do you like and why?
- What poems confuse you and why?
- What words does the poet use that you think are interesting?

- What pictures form in your mind as you read? How does the writer create these images?
- Do you notice any literary devices that the poet uses (think of the Poet's Toolbox)? Does the poet use a particular device repeatedly?

To conclude the discussion of the poet in expert groups, students reflect individually about the poet and his or her poems. The literature circle discussions provide students with opportunities to build on their own comprehension by including the varied interpretations of others. When a student reconciles his or her own interpretations with those of others in the expert group, his or her critical thinking is strengthened. Next, students write responses to the following prompts, preparing for their upcoming roles in their home groups:

- What do you want to share about your poet's writing in your home group? Draft a list of 5 to 10 points that you will communicate.
- Choose a poem that you would like to share with your home group, providing your reasons for selecting it.

Next, students meet in their home groups, where each member shares his or her insights about the poet's work. Students are focused by the notes that they took during expert group discussions and by their final reflections. Each home-group member concludes his or her presentation by reading aloud the poem that he or she selected. When each home group finishes, students then enjoy a 30-minute SSR period, during which time they may read any of the poetry anthologies available in the classroom library.

Wrapping Up
Reading books, poems, and magazines is a daily occurrence in language arts classrooms, even outside poetry workshop. The poet study, however, is a formal activity in which students read and discuss classic and contemporary poetry—analyzing and synthesizing what they have discovered about poetry writing.

ACTIVITY 12

Objectives
- To provide students with experiences in which they critically read and write about a poet's writing
- To give students opportunities to explore and enjoy poets' works, reading poetry as writers

Procedure
The teacher chooses an important, developmentally appropriate theme for middle school students such as "respect for others," "becoming your best," "overcoming obstacles," "showing courage," or "accepting differences." Students are assigned the task of finding one poem that encapsulates the theme chosen by the teacher. On the day scheduled for this activity, students bring to class copies of poems that they have selected. In small groups, each student reads aloud a poem, explaining its meaning and how it fits the theme. This serves as prewriting for the drafting step.

Next, students are instructed to write two paragraphs in which they reflect on the poems. They plan and write their individual reflections after synthesizing what they have discussed.

The following example demonstrates how one student transacts with the poem "Just Me" by Tom Krause (2001) (see Appendix D), sharing interpretations, making evaluations, and making connections among herself, the poem, and the theme—responsibility for one's actions. The student then communicates her interpretation of the poem in writing, manifesting her critical thinking.

> I chose the poem "Just Me" because it shows that you need to take responsibility for your actions, and that the author became his best by not blaming others for what he did. He learned that he should give more respect to his teammates and that there will always be someone better than him at something. Tom learned to stop being selfish and learned to depend on others more.
>
> It fits into our theme because he started to take responsibility for his actions. Once Tom realized his behavior was hurting himself and others, he knew that he could work on his game and become the best he could be. He started giving respect to others and showing courage by working toward his goal even when better players challenged him. Responsibility and respect are things the kids in our grade are working on with the help of our teachers, parents, and other adults who care about us.
>
> —SHANNON, AGE 11

Wrapping Up

This activity compels students to read poetry in search of a poem that has personal meaning. It serves three instructional goals: (1) promoting independent reading, (2) encouraging thoughtful reflection on the meaning of a poem in reference to the chosen theme, and (3) communicating meaning in writing. Figure 7 shows a rubric that may be used to evaluate students' interpretation and analysis of their poems.

FIGURE 7
Rubric for Poem Search

Advanced—4	Proficient—3	Basic—2	Below Basic—1
Reflection is a thorough explanation of what the poem means to the student and how it fits the theme.	Reflection is a general explanation of what the poem means to the student and how it fits the theme.	Reflection is a vague explanation of what the poem means to the student and how it fits the theme.	Reflection is not related to the prompt.

Objectives
• To compose poetry as a response to learning in all curricular areas and to reading a text
• To provide an alternative assessment in all curricular areas

Procedure
At a presentation by Barry Lane, author of *After the End* (1993), we were introduced to the format of a how-to-be poem. Lane defines this poem as a "list poem" that allows writers to "effectively play around with specific facts" (p. 59). First, the teacher directs students to list facts about a particular topic. Once brainstorming is completed, students arrange these details into poems by using what they have learned about the craft of poetry as shown in the following example.

How to Be a Surfer
Paddle
Against waves
Like a kayaker
Fighting white water rapids
Pull yourself up
Be the wave and
Ride as one
Be flung off your faithful board
Thrown beneath the surface
To be
Suspended
In
Calm
Quiet
Before you surface to hear
The crashing and sucking
Throw back your hair
Find your surfboard
Try again
Ride beneath the ocean's roof
This time around
Through the tunnel of ocean

Ride
Through
The
Tunnel
Of
Ocean
For
Ever

—JAYNE, AGE 12

As reading and writing teachers, we also have used this format as an alternative assessment to monitor students' comprehension after reading. This alternative assessment and rubric afford valuable insight about students' literal and interpretive comprehension. For example, after reading *Get on Board: The Story of the Underground Railroad* by Jim Haskins (1993) and *Warriors Don't Cry* by Melba Beals (1994), books about slavery and the U.S. civil rights movement, students create how-to-be poems. Students are required to focus on historical facts about the era, communicating their comprehension of the text.

The following poems demonstrate students' comprehension of the texts they read. Both students include details about the historical eras that the poems address—slavery and the U.S. civil rights movement. In addition, one student provides her interpretation about what it was like to be a slave, and another student offers hers about Melba Beals, one of the famous Little Rock Nine (the first black students to integrate a southern U.S. high school in Arkansas).

How to Be a Slave
Taken from your country
And sold like an animal
Work for no pay night and day
Slavery, slavery.

No choice for a job
No complaints allowed
No rights
Slavery, slavery.

Watch your children be sold
Suffer abuse

No freedom
Slavery, slavery.

Sing to ease your sorrows
Never give up

Run, run, leave everything
Trusting strangers to help you escape
Tracks to freedom—Underground Railroad
Free, free at last.

—ANNA, AGE 11

How to Be Melba Beals
Brown vs. Board of Education
Ordering integration
is passed.
Rush and sign up...
Too fast.

Now scared of the pain,
Knowing the white people will go insane!

There is no turning back now,
'Cause you have made yourself a vow
To continue.

So hold your head high,
Let the hateful, nasty words fly,
And walk right on by.
Have a soldier to protect you from harm.
To help you,
the victim of the whites' anger,
From their deadly alarm

Acid is thrown in your face
Just because of your race.
All you can do is wash it out,

Because no matter what
No one will do anything,
There is no doubt!

Attend interview after interview,
There is little else you can do
To explain what you are going through.

Have strength in your mind,
No matter how unkind
The white people are!

One white man helps you,
You are very thankful,
For this is a brave thing to do!

Mom loses her job
Your family does not just sob,
They fight back
Because this family does not want to lack...
anything.

Make it through the year,
You have taken as much as you can bear!

You do not hold a grudge
Against all white men.
You get married to one yourself,
Because you do not judge!

You have a strong mind,
Determined to do what no other black has done before,
You think to yourself
I am a warrior,
And warriors don't cry!

—KERRY, AGE 11

Wrapping Up

It was immediately clear to us that this poem format also could be used as an alternative assessment across the curriculum. After students have studied or researched curricular topics in social studies, science, health, music, and math, they draft a list of important facts and organize them into how-to-be poems. After the completion of an environmental unit focusing on the interaction of living and nonliving things, for example, students compose how-to-be poems that communicate what they have learned. Figure 8 shows examples of creative products that communicate students' knowledge. Figure 9 presents a rubric that may be used to evaluate students' comprehension of text.

FIGURE 8
How-to-Be Poems From an Environmental Unit

How to be A Friend of The Earth
by Mokhter Belair

Plant more trees
conserve your energy
protest against de forestation
How to Be A friend
How to Be A friend
don't waste your water
we don't have enough
Why poach animals
they have rights too
How to Be A friend
How to Be A friend
don't litter, it's ugly
why cut down trees
or make fires
How to Be A friend
How to Be A friend
plant a garden, they are pretty
Use the AC, only when needed
recycle your paper, glass too
How to be a friend
How to be a friend to me

(continued)

FIGURE 8 (continued)
How-to-Be Poems From an Environmental Unit

How to be A friend to the Earth
by Becky ONeill

Recycle,
Ride a bicycle,
Put trash in the right place,
It will give you safer playing space,
don't you hunt you better not,
global warming makes it hot,
feed the horses
In fresh air,
Help the Environment with some care.

FIGURE 9
Rubric for How-to-Be-Poem

Advanced–4	Proficient–3	Basic–2	Below Basic–1
Accurate, specific explanation of thinking, offering thorough support of interpretation	Sufficient explanation of thinking, offering some support of interpretation	Vague or somewhat general explanation of thinking that lacks support of interpretation	Superficial explanation of thinking that does not show an interpretation
Shows strong understanding of text by including details and personal insights of the topic	Shows an adequate understanding of texts with some details and personal insights	Shows limited understanding of text with few details and personal insights	Shows a lack of understanding of text with minimal details and personal insights

Objectives
- To compose poetry that demonstrates comprehension of a text (an alternative assessment)
- To communicate personal understanding of significant life events
- To activate prior knowledge
- To provide a basis for connections with text

Procedure
A found poem is formed by using words "found" in a text. Students choose words, phrases, and sentences that stand out for them, and arrange the selections into lines and stanzas to create a poem. The following example shows the writer's understanding of theme. After reading the short story "The War of the Wall" by Toni Cade Bambara (1994), students write found poems, focusing on the theme of respect.

Quality, Not Quantity

Humor, respect, and kindness are wonderful traits
No bragging would be nice too
Stay true and blue
You must listen and be cool
Be generous, but don't change a thing
Don't think you're better than another,
I'll think you're honest then
Just lean on me, and I'll be your friend
Keep your own personality, just the way you are
Make smart decisions, and you'll go far
Don't talk about people behind their backs
You never know—the tables might turn

—CAITLIN, AGE 12

In the following student poems, the purpose of the found poem transcends mere comprehension of the written word; instead, it becomes a vehicle for adolescents to make sense of events in their world and communicate their perspectives to others.

Students were eager to discuss the horrific events of September 11, 2001. In the middle school classroom, students typically are invested in the discussions that concern their feelings and opinions. To channel their emotional responses to the

September 11 tragedy, students read newspaper articles about it. The teacher directed students to highlight the words, phrases, and sentences in the article that struck them as they read. Students composed found poems that demonstrate their personal responses to this event:

War Zone
Unimaginable, unspeakable carnage
9:40 a.m. the second plane hit the Towers
Eyewitnesses recall seeing people jump
A man and woman held hands
As they jumped out of the building

Two feet of soot everywhere
No eyebrows, no hair
I count all the dead people
Dazed New Yorker
Numb with shock
Looks like a war zone

—GABRIELLE, AGE 13

WTC's Last Day
World Trade Center, smoking rubble
800 people still missing from the Pentagon
Ferries carried dead across the river
Three cab companies ripped out their seats to carry the dead
I lost count of all the dead people I saw
259 uniformed officers still unaccounted for
The highest state of alert
Death toll may not be known for weeks
Unimaginable, unspeakable carnage
A man and a woman held hands as they plunged to their
    deaths
Eyewitness recalls seeing people
Jumping out of buildings
Dazed New Yorkers

—PATRICK, AGE 13

In a reading and writing classroom, the found-poem procedure can be used before reading a novel to activate prior knowledge and to provide a basis for connections that students will make as they read the text. For this variation of found poems, the teacher searches for picture books that match the instructional goals to promote literal and interpretative reading comprehension. For example, students write found poems before reading *Where the Red Fern Grows* by Wilson Rawls (1984) in which the protagonist's relationship with his coon dogs motivates much of his behavior and advances the plot. Students also read the following picture books that focus on the relationship between humans and animals:

Amigo by Byrd Baylor

Annie and the Wild Animals by Jan Brett

Leah's Pony by Elizabeth Friedrich

I Want a Dog by Dayal Kaur Khalsa

My Buddy by Audrey Osofsky

My Jack by Iza Trapani

The Tenth Good Thing About Barney by Judith Viorst

After reading one of the assigned picture books, students brainstorm with a partner, jotting down key words, phrases, and sentences found in the text. Each pair creates a found poem to demonstrate their understanding and interpretation of the relationship between humans and animals, readying students for reading the text. For example, the following found poem "Daydreaming About Dogs," written in response to *I Want a Dog* (Khalsa, 1999), communicates two students' understanding of how a character thinks, acts, and feels when he or she desires a dog. The conflict in this book is similar to that of the protagonist in *Where the Red Fern Grows* (Rawls, 1984), which students will experience when they read the novel.

Daydreaming About Dogs

Dog biscuits

Drawings of dogs

Daydreaming about dogs

Birthday presents

Roller-skate

Taxi

Daydreaming about dogs

Try, try and try again

Training

Leash
Daydreaming about dogs
Garbage cans
Obey
Care
Daydreaming about dogs

—SARA AND KELLY, AGE 13

In the following poem written in response to *The Tenth Good Thing About Barney* (Viorst, 1976), students convey their understanding of a character's conflict when a beloved pet dies, again similar to that in *Where the Red Fern Grows*:

Ten Good Things

Barney died last Friday
I cried, and I didn't watch television
I didn't eat my chicken or even the chocolate pudding
I should think of ten good things about Barney
I thought, and I thought, and thought of good things about
    Barney
And I told good things about Barney
Those are all good things, said mother, but I just count nine
I miss Barney
Will Barney change too? I asked
Barney was brave
Yes, but now I have another
Barney is in the ground and he's helping grow flowers
Barney died last Friday
I miss him

—ANTHONY, AGE 12, AND SAM, AGE 13

The following found poem shares a title with the picture book *My Buddy* (Osofsky, 1994). In this poem, students express their understanding of the close bond that develops between a pet and a boy. The loving relationship that is addressed readily connects to Billy's relationship with his two coon hounds in *Where the Red Fern Grows*.

My Buddy

Best Friends.
Never gets mad.
Never runs off with another boy.
Always listens.
My golden retriever.
Looks like the sun is always shining on him.
His big brown eyes are sweet as a smile
He's more than a friend
He's my arms and legs
He helps me
Buddy is my wish come true
He is special
Loving and smart
Star of puppy kindergarten
I never gave up
I wanted Buddy more
We belong together
Buddy looked me in the eye and obeyed
He learned to trust me
I learned to trust him
We were a team
My new friend
Buddy only listens to me
Buddy was a pro
Wagging his tail
Handy, smart, funny
Just one of the guys
Quietest one in the class
He's just happy to play with me
We're a team
Buddy is my best friend
He knows I'm his best friend too
He gives me sloppy kisses.
I give him hugs back.
Whatever we do, we do together
He's my buddy.

—Cassi and Marisa, age 13

Wrapping Up

The variations of this activity serve as alternative assessments in which students communicate their thinking. The student examples in this section clearly demonstrate that poetry writing can be used to activate prior knowledge, make connections to text, and convey meaning about personal experiences.

Objectives
• To communicate reader's interpretation of a character based on the details from the text and the reader's evaluations and connections
• To compose poetry that illustrates characterization

Procedure
Language arts teachers implement various instructional strategies so students as readers can communicate their interpretations of, evaluations of, and connections to text. Several practical approaches—dialogue journals, double-entry journals, and literature circles—facilitate the types of reader responses that demonstrate critical thinking. Writing poetry also affords students a vehicle to communicate their critical thinking about text.

A character poem is written to communicate the reader's interpretation of a character, including his or her evaluations of and connections to the text. Teachers should adjust the requirements to suit their instructional goals. For example, when reading *The Cay* by Theodore Taylor (1987), a goal for students is to recognize, evaluate, and connect to the character's change in perspective. Phillip, the protagonist, experiences a rite of passage and students' interpretation of, evaluation of, and connection to this transformation becomes the basis for a poem. The description and rubric in Figures 10 and 11 demonstrate how one teacher adapted the idea of a character poem to meet her purposes.

FIGURE 10
Rite-of-Passage Poem: The Cay

In *The Cay*, Phillip experiences a transformation. His perspective about life changes, owing mostly to his interaction with Timothy. Write a poem capturing the "before" Phillip—the rising action—and the "after" Phillip—the falling action.

Requirements

Focus
• Show Phillip's rite of passage.

Content and Organization
• Your poem should have three stanzas.

> Stanza 1
> Describe the "before" Phillip.
> Include at least three direct quotations—10 to 12 lines of poetry.

> Stanza 2
> Describe the climax.
> Include at least two direct quotations—5 to 8 lines of poetry.

> Stanza 3
> Describe the "after" Phillip.
> Include at least three direct quotations.
> Write 10 to 12 lines of poetry.

Style
• Include at least three figures of speech: simile, metaphor, personification, alliteration, and so on.
• Include at least two magic 3's (see chapter 4, page 55)

Conventions
• Proofread your poem for spelling, grammar, punctuation, and capitalization.

Following Directions
• Submit a final draft typed in a legible font.
• Include graphics to convey Phillip's change.

FIGURE 11
Rubric for Rite-of-Passage Poem

Focus
• Illustrate Phillip's rite of passage and change in perspective.

| Advanced—4 | Proficient—3 | Basic—2 | Below Basic—1 |

Content and Organization
• Three Stanzas
> Stanza 1—Describe the "before" Phillip; include at least three direct quotations and 10 to 12 lines.
>
> Stanza 2—Describe the climax; include at least two direct quotations and 5 to 8 lines
>
> Stanza 3—Describes the "after" Phillip; includes at least three direct quotations and 10 to 12 lines

| Advanced—24 | Proficient—20 | Basic—16 | Below Basic—12 |

Style
• Use at least three figures of speech.
• Include at least two magic 3's.

| Advanced—12 | Proficient—9 | Basic—6 | Below Basic—3 |

Conventions
• Use correct spelling, grammar, punctuation, and capitalization.

| Advanced—12 | Proficient—9 | Basic—6 | Below Basic—3 |

Following Directions
• Submit final draft in a legible font.
• Include graphics to convey Phillip's change.

| Advanced—8 | Proficient—6 | Basic—4 | Below Basic—2 |

_____ points earned/60 possible

Wrapping Up

In this alternative assessment, students clearly comprehend, evaluate, and connect to the novel as evinced in the following rite-of-passage poems:

Opened
Complete darkness.
No light, no food, and no friendship.
Black equals bad.
The world shut out.
One island, two different people.
"I wondered if he knew anything,

Or if he was just a stupid black man..."
Hatred flowed through Phillip.
"I knew he made a mistake in bringing us ashore..."
Equivalent, not to Phillip.
"I reminded him, again, stupid black man, I couldn't see..."
Racism ate their friendship.

The lid opened.
Blackness still there, tight as a blanket.
A light shone, a sign, directing Phillip out.
"You ugly black man, I won't do it! You can't even spell..."
The force, fright, and freedom of the slap.
Phillip was opened.
"Can you call me Phillip instead of young boss?"
Equivalent, yes.

The storm came.
Enormous, brutal, and frightening.
"Timothy was taking the full punishment of the storm..."
True friends, gone like the wind.
"Timothy was dead."
Cried, dug, and buried.
Take care of him God, he was good to me..."
Phillip saw Timothy's beauty,
The day he was buried.
"He felt neither white nor black..."
Bonds were built, friendship formed.
Black and white stood no more.

—Jena, age 12

No Color
The deep darkness of Phillip's past.
His mind controls his every movement.
"You're saving all the water for yourself," Phillip yelled.
All alone on a desolate cay,
While surrounded by the comforting fish and water.
"I'm blind, I'm blind," Phillip screamed.

Phillip let anger go, but his mind told him not to.
The coal black darkness was a sheet over Phillip's eyes.
"Timothy, I'm blind. I can't see to work."
Phillip's stubbornness is like a gnat,
It follows him until he swats it away.

"You ugly black man! I won't do it!
You're stupid, you can't even spell..."
The slap, an alarm clock waking him up, after an almost
   sleepless night.
"Can you call me Phillip instead of young boss?"
Friendship is a bond, holding two people together.
The soldier of friendship,
Strives through the brutal war, unscathed.

"You went into the water. You scared me, Timothy."
A new beginning, the start of a new friendship.
Like a fire in the wind, the anger and hatred were extinguished.
"As my feet touched the ground, Timothy hugged me..."
A smile on his bold face,
Filled with confidence and happiness,
Gave Phillip a warm feeling, although blind.
"Old Timothy of Charlotte Amalie was dead."
Death, a boat silently coming up the river,
Finally is going to pick up Timothy.
The tears slowly run down Phillip's face,
Each are filled with pain and sorrow.

—ANDREA, AGE 12

ACTIVITY 16   Personal-Response Poem

Objectives
• To respond to poetry
• To provide students with opportunities to communicate personal meaning about a poem

Procedure
This activity originates from the use of double-entry journals as a response to reading in our classrooms and from an adaptation of Heard's (1999) "call-and-response" (p. 33), which we combined to form the personal response poem.

We use "I Hear America Singing" by Walt Whitman and "I, Too" by Langston Hughes (see Appendix D). These poems show two poets' different views of living in the United States. To begin, students read their choice of the two teacher-selected poems. Familiar with the double-entry journal as a response to reading, students record their feelings, connections, reactions, and evaluations about the poem next to its lines and stanzas. This task serves as the prewriting step in the writing process. Then, students draft poems using what they have learned about the craft of writing poetry. The poems communicate students' understanding and interpretations of the text. The following students' responses generate varied interpretations.

America Mine and Yours
(in response to "I Hear America Singing")

I hear the singing of the mechanics,
    masons, boatmen, and
      shoemakers
Different colors,
But all equal,
Black and white,
Chocolate and vanilla,
Different color,
Same purpose,
Different song
Same rhythm,
The day belongs,
To all,
Not one,

We are America,
All equal,
Singing in,
The same harmony,
America

—Chris, age 11

— 85 —

Tomorrow

(in response to "I, Too")

All blame
Jealousy
And hatred will be gone
Tomorrow
My inner beauty will rise up and shine brighter than the sun
Tomorrow
They will be ashamed
Because tomorrow
They'll see
The inner beauty that gleams
Inside of me

—Kayleen, age 12

Wrapping Up

Students respond to poetry by writing poetry—a tangible sign that they are experiencing, interpreting, and responding to literature by taking an aesthetic stance (Rosenblatt, 1965). This activity positions students to interact with the text to make personal meaning.

ACTIVITY 17   Two-Voice Poem

Objectives
- To compose poetry as a response to learning in all curricular areas and to reading of text
- To provide an alternative assessment in all curricular areas

Procedure
Joyful Noise: Poems for Two Voices (Fleischman, 1989), a collection of two-voice poems inspired this activity. A two-voice poem appears as two separate poems printed side by side on a page. Two speakers read aloud the lines—simultaneously if the text appears on the same line in both columns, or separately if the text appears on a line in only one column.

Before students write two-voice poems, it is beneficial for them, in pairs, to read aloud examples from *Joyful Noise* so they become familiar with the format and its effects. Students should read a few examples aloud to the whole class; then, the teacher may highlight the unique style and format. Initial attempts at composing two-voice poems are more successful when students work in pairs because speaking and listening play a significant part in drafting.

One variation is a response to reading *Animal Farm* by George Orwell (1990). Students work in pairs to write a two-voice poem, sharing their interpretations of *Animal Farm* and the historical speech "I Have a Dream" by Martin Luther King, Jr. (1963). First, during a class discussion, students highlight significant aspects of Old Major's speech to the barnyard animals in *Animal Farm*. After reading this fictitious speech, the class reads aloud "I Have a Dream." Students work in pairs to compare both speeches, noting similarities and differences.

The graphic organizers for a two-voice poem (see Appendix H) serve as a prewriting instrument to organize students' thinking about both speeches. One of the graphic organizers taps students' understanding of the texts, and the other focuses students' attention on the rhetorical tools—alliteration, repetition, metaphor, rhetorical questions, and allusion—that speakers use to convey messages. After students complete the process of drafting, conferencing, and revising, the published pieces demonstrate their comprehension of the text as well as rhetorical devices. (See the student example on page 88.)

Figure 12 on page 89 presents a rubric that may be used to evaluate the two-voice poem.

Two Different Worlds

(in response to *Animal Farm* and "I Have A Dream")

I have a dream
One day
We will kick Mr. Jones
Out of the farm

One day
All animals will be
Overfed

One day
We animals will kick
Out the humans

One day
Animals won't be
Killed if they're useless

One day
The fields won't be
Full of weeds

One day
The poor roofing
Will be replaced

One day
My dream will be fulfilled
One day all animals will
Be treated equally

I have a dream
One day
Every man will be treated
Equally

One day
Little black children and
Little white children will
Play together happily

One day
Dark and desolate valleys
Of segregation will come
Together

One day
Freedom will ring

One day
Former slaves and former
Slave owners will be
Friends

One day
Our nation will rise up
And live out the true
Meaning of its creed

One day
My dream will be fulfilled
One day all humans will
Be treated equally

—BECKIE AND LEANN, AGE 12

FIGURE 12 Rubric for Two-Voice Poem			
Advanced—4	Proficient—3	Basic—2	Below Basic—1
Accurate, specific explanation of thinking, offering thorough support of interpretation	Sufficient explanation of thinking, offering some support of interpretation	Vague or somewhat general explanation of thinking that lacks support of interpretation	Superficial explanation of thinking that does not show an interpretation
Shows true understanding of rhetorical devices	Shows general understanding of rhetorical devices	Shows limited understanding of rhetorical devices	Shows a lack of understanding of rhetorical devices

Wrapping Up

The two-voice poem format is a valuable alternative assessment for responding to reading. In this activity, students respond to text, conveying their understanding. The nontraditional format encourages students to make connections between texts, strengthening their interpretations of both texts.

This activity also may be adapted to have students write one column about themselves and one column about a book character, noting similarities in lines that are spoken together and differences in those spoken separately. By making connections between self and text, students strengthen their comprehension of text because personal experience enhances understanding.

Once students have an understanding of and comfort with poetry writing, teachers are empowered to extend student responses to include poetry as a means to communicate learning. It is important for teachers to provide alternative assessments to gauge student learning, meeting the varied learning styles of students. As the activities in this chapter demonstrate, students can communicate their learning in ways other than traditional assessments. The poetry writing reveals the writer's knowledge and understanding, and it can be powerful for the reader.

AFTERWORD

As reading and writing teachers, our fundamental goal is to develop lifelong readers, writers, and learners—students who view themselves as writers for readers and readers who write. This understanding renders language learning that is meaningful to students. Meaningful learning occurs in poetry workshop as students are engaged in reading, composing, listening to, and discussing poetry.

Poetry workshop is a valuable, research-supported practice to adopt in the middle school reading and writing classroom. Zemelman et al. (1998) define quality literacy instruction as including the following:

- Time for independent reading
- Student choice
- Exposure to wide and rich range of literature
- Social and collaborative activities with much discussion and interaction
- Student ownership
- Classroom time spent on writing whole and original pieces
- Instruction in and support for all stages of writing process
- Teacher modeling
- Writing for real audiences
- Publishing for the class and for wider communities
- Active exchange and valuing of students' ideas
- Collaborative small-group work
- Conferences and peer critiquing that gives responsibility for improvement to authors
- Brief informal oral responses as students work
- Encouragement of risk taking and honest expression. (pp. 54, 82)

These elements of good literacy instruction are alive in poetry workshop. It is evident when reading student poems, listening to and participating in class discussions, and conferencing with student writers that meaningful learning occurs in our classrooms.

When we first implemented poetry-writing activities in our language arts classes, the success of poetry workshop was apparent immediately as evidenced in our students' writing. Furthermore, we consider our students' writing the best assessment of our instructional practices. We are confident that as other teachers take the first steps to initiate poetry writing in their classrooms, they will find similar success.

Poet's Toolbox

Figure of speech	Definition	Example
Metaphor	A comparison of two unlike objects, not using the words *like* or *as*. Even though the objects are not alike physically, they have one quality in common, just enough to make a comparison	Her mind is a computer. The inky-black sky was home to bats (the color of the sky is compared to the color of ink).
Simile	A comparison of two unlike objects, using the words *like* or *as*	Some raindrops are as big as nickels.
Hyperbole	Exaggeration	Aunt Mary's head was the size of the barn after I complimented her cooking.
Personification	Giving human qualities to something that is not human	Rain tickles my face, trying to cheer me up.
Alliteration	The repetition of the initial sounds in words	The big rain rattles and roars. Silly circus seals.
Onomatopoeia	The use of words that imitate sounds	Hiss, crash, buzz.
Imagery	Descriptive language used to recreate sensory experience; words that show what the speaker sees, hears, smells, touches, or tastes	Snow fell like coconut flakes, fluttering to the cold ground as gracefully as feathers.

Type of poem	Definition	Example
Lyric poem	Expresses the observations and feelings of a single experience in the life of the speaker	"Stopping by Woods on a Snowy Evening" by Robert Frost; *The Napping House* by Audrey Wood
Free verse	Verse with no regular rhyme scheme or rhythmic pattern	"Mother to Son" by Langston Hughes
Narrative poem	Tells a true or imaginative story and has character, setting, plot, theme, and point of view. It tells events in chronological order. Many narrative poems tell stories of famous heroes	"Paul Revere's Ride" by Henry Longfellow; *Lady Bugatti* by Joyce Maxner

Mystery Slips

Adjectives

watery	silent	embracing	metallic
silky	nervous	burning	tranquil
tiny	timid	thin	starry
wide	fresh	sweaty	chapped
sour	splendid	charred	awkward
golden	short	rippling	crimson
chocolate	cheerful	exquisite	electric
blooming	melting	spotted	murky
turbulent	shiny	sizzling	curt
tired	malicious	slippery	staccato
agitated	boundless	freckled	gloomy
soaring	calm	unknown	titanic
awaiting	weak	furry	sly
smooth	vanishing	enormous	silver
uncertain	cold	dismal	pungent
rough	hot	sudsy	opaque
rigid	jagged	fuzzy	gleaming
miserable	surprised	meager	explosive
glittering	shadowy	fleeting	nonchalant
noisy	unruffled	uneven	raging
loquacious	uncanny	chalky	anxious
plastic	skinny	coarse	regal
split	graceful	dazzling	chaotic
scary	hidden	secretive	

Nouns

tears	song	hockey	icicle
heart	petals	umbrella	hugs
balloon	darkness	trash	silence
stars	shadow	dog	crowd
butterfly	dream	report card	blur
diamonds	holiday	student	chair
window	love	teacher	loneliness
moon	hope	sky	puddle
sun	night	window	jeans
smile	forest	leaves	color
daylight	ocean	geyser	flood
pencil	jewel	abyss	sailboat
tree	bedlam	gate	ghost
flower	air	kite	oasis
cafeteria	kiss	siren	anger
rainbow	mountain	fence	joy
bubbles	clouds	castle	weekend
music	book	flag	applause
sea	ring	nightmare	ski trip
hat	ice	courage	metal
tune	snowflake	beach	fireworks
raindrops	hands	rose	scream
eyes	sand	rock	wave
snow	emeralds	ruby	tide
dragon	fear	friendship	pebbles

Imagery Graphic Organizer

Hear

See

Smell

A Busy Place

Taste

Touch

Poems for Personal Response

I, Too

I, too, sing America.

I am the darker brother,
They send me to eat in the kitchen
When company comes,
But I laugh
And eat well,
And grow strong.

Tomorrow,
I'll sit at the table
When company comes.
Nobody'll dare
Say to me,
"Eat in the kitchen,"
Then.

Besides,
They'll see how beautiful I am
And be ashamed—

I, too, am America.

—LANGSTON HUGHES

From The Collected Poems of Langston Hughes, *copyright © 1994 by the Estate of Langston Hughes.
Used with permission of Alfred A Knopf, Random House, Inc.*

I Hear America Singing

I hear America singing, the varied
carols I hear:

Those of mechanics—each one singing
his, as it should be, blithe and strong:
The carpenter singing his, as he
measures his plank or beam,

The mason singing his, as he makes
ready for work, or leaves off work;

The boatman singing what belongs to
him in his boat—the deckhand singing
on the steamboat deck;

The shoemaker singing as he sits on
his bench—the hatter singing as he
stands;

The wood cutter's song—the
ploughboy's on his way in the
morning, or at noon intermission, or
at sundown;

The delicious singing of the mother—
Or of the young wife at work—or of
the girl sewing or washing—

Each singing what belongs to him or
her and to no one else;
The day what belongs to the day—at
night, the party of young fellows,
robust, friendly,

Singing, with open mouths, their
strong melodious songs.

   —WALT WHITMAN

From Whitman, W. (circa 1900). Leaves of Grass. Philadelphia: David McKay.

Just Me

From the time I was little I knew I was great
'cause the people would tell me "You'll make it—just wait."
But they never did tell me how great I would be
If I ever played someone who was greater than me.

When I'm in the backyard, I'm king with the ball.
To swish all those baskets with no sweat at all.
But all of a sudden there's a man in my face
Who doesn't seem to realize that I'm king of this place.

So the pressure gets to me; I rush with the ball.
My passes to teammates could go through the wall.
My jumpers not falling, my dribbles not sure.
My hand is not steady, my eye is not pure.

The fault is my teammates—they don't understand.
The fault is my coaches—what a terrible plan.
The fault is the call by that blind referee.
But the fault is not mine; I'm the greatest, you see.

Then finally it hit me when I started to see
that the face in the mirror looked exactly like me.
It wasn't my teammates who were dropping the ball
and it wasn't my coach shooting bricks at the wall.

That face in the mirror that was always so great
had some room for improvement instead of just hate.
So I stopped blaming others and started to grow.
My play got much better and it started to show.

And all of my teammates didn't seem quite so bad.
I learned to depend on the good friends I had.
Now I like myself better since I started to see
that I was lousy being great—I'm much better being me.

—TOM KRAUSE

From Krause, T. (2001). Touching Hearts—Touching Greatness: Stories From a Coach That Touch Your Heart and Inspire Your Soul. Kansas City, MO: Andrews McMeel. Used with permission of the author.

Professional Publishing Opportunities

The following publications accept student submissions. It is important to check with the contest or publication about guidelines for submitting writing, and it is suggested that a self-addressed, stamped envelope and a cover letter be submitted with all works.

Stone Soup
PO Box 83, Santa Cruz, California 95063, USA
www.stonesoup.com

Creative Kids
PO Box 8813, Waco, Texas 76714-8813, USA
www.prufrock.com/prufrock_jm_createkids.cfm

Celebration of Young Poets by Creative Communication
There are two deadlines, spring and fall. Students may enter their poems either online at www.poeticpower.com or mail entries to Creative Communication, 90 North 100 East, Logan, Utah 84321, USA.

Rubric for Class Poetry Book

Name _____

Title: _____

Content

- The book will include 8 to 10 original poems, demonstrating the use of poet's tools.
- Each poem will have a title.
- Poems will be typed in lines and stanzas—not paragraphs.

Advanced—40   Proficient—35   Basic—30

Organization

- Cover page: title, author's name
- Title page: title, author's name, publishing company, city of publication
- Copyright page: Copyright © year
- Dedication page
- Table of contents
- Illustrations or clip art included for each poem

0 to 2 omissions/errors—20   3 to 6 omissions/errors—15   More than 6 omissions/errors—10

Conventions

- Spelling, grammar, punctuation

Advanced—20   Proficient—15   Basic—10

Neatness and Following Directions

Well done—10   Needs improvement—5

_____ points earned/90 possible points

Comments:

Poetry Assessment— Take-Home Assignment

Name _____

Due Date _____

Directions:

• Answer in complete sentences, using your daily writing journal with the poetry drafts.

• You will need to use sticky notes in your journal to mark the poems that you are discussing; label the sticky notes with the test question number.

• You will need a highlighter to highlight the lines that you are discussing in your poem.

1. Did your feeling about poetry reading and poetry writing change in any way after you completed poetry workshop? If yes, explain how it has changed. If no, explain why you believe it did not. Be thorough—support your explanation.

4	3	2	1	0
Accurate, specific explanation of thinking, offering thorough support of opinion	General explanation of thinking, offering some support of opinion	Inaccurate, vague, or incomplete explanation that lacks support of opinion	Somewhat related to the question, but does not answer the specific question	Illegible or no answer

2. In your daily writing journal, find a poem that contains figurative language.

- Place a sticky note on the page where the poem is and write #2.
- Highlight the line in the poem that contains the example.
- In the space below, identify what the device is (e.g., simile, personification, etc.) and explain how it made your poem stronger.

4	3	2	1	0
Accurate, specific explanation of thinking, offering thorough support of opinion; shows true understanding of figurative language	General explanation of thinking, offering some support of opinion; shows general understanding of figurative language	Inaccurate, vague, or incomplete explanation that lacks support of opinion; shows limited understanding of figurative language	Somewhat related to the question, but does not answer the specific question; shows a lack of understanding of figurative language	Illegible or no answer

3. Find another poem that contains figurative language.

- Place a sticky note on the page where the poem is and write #3.
- Highlight the line in the poem that contains the example.
- In the space below, identify the device (e.g., simile, personification, etc.) and explain how it made your poem stronger.

4	3	2	1	0
Accurate, specific explanation of thinking, offering thorough support of opinion; shows true understanding of figurative language	General explanation of thinking, offering some support of opinion; shows general understanding of figurative language	Inaccurate, vague, or incomplete explanation that lacks support of opinion; shows limited understanding of figurative language	Somewhat related to the question, but does not answer the specific question; shows a lack of understanding of figurative language	Illegible or no answer

4. Revision of poetry writing is important to the writer and reader of poetry. In your daily writing journal, find a poem that shows revision.
   - Place a sticky note on the page where the poem is, and draw a star to mark the poem.
   - In the space below, explain the revisions that you made and why you made them.
   - Discuss how it made your poem stronger. Be thorough in support of your explanation.

4	3	2	1	0
Accurate, specific explanation of thinking, offering thorough support of opinion; shows true understanding of revision	General explanation of thinking, offering some support of opinion; shows general understanding of revision	Inaccurate, vague, or incomplete explanation that lacks support of opinion; shows limited understanding of revision	Somewhat related to the question, but does not answer the specific question; shows a lack of understanding of revision	Illegible or no answer

Two-Voice Poem Graphic Organizer

Analyzing Speeches—Style

Rhetorical tools	Martin Luther King's "I Have a Dream" (King, 1963)	Old Major's Speech from *Animal Farm* (Orwell, 1990)
Alliteration Examples of repetition of the same consonant sounds		
Repetition Key words or phrases that are repeated for emphasis		
Metaphor List comparisons that help listeners "envision" meaning. • Example: "Let our dreams soar on wings of optimism!"		
Rhetorical questions List questions that are for effect rather than to be answered. • Example: "Will we stand now on the brink of history or will we let the moment pass unchallenged?"		

Allusion Find examples of allusion (a reference to a person, place, or thing in history or another work of literature).		

Analyzing Speeches—Content

Basic Structure	Martin Luther King's "I Have a Dream"	Old Major's Speech from *Animal Farm*
Describe the present situation. Who is benefiting under the current conditions? How?		
Prove unfairness. Who is suffering under the current conditions? How?		
Provide a vision of a better way. What would conditions be like if the conditions were fairer than they are now?		
Call for action. What must be done to achieve fairer conditions?		

REFERENCES

Atwell, N. (1987). *In the middle: Writing, reading, and learning with adolescents.* Portsmouth, NH: Heinemann.

Brogan, K., & Brewer, R. (2002). *Writer's market.* Cincinnati, OH: F & W Publications.

Carey, M.A. (1989). *Poetry: Starting from scratch.* Lincoln, NE: Foundation Books.

Ebsensen, B.J. (1995). *A celebration of bees: Helping children write poetry.* New York: Henry Holt.

Graves, D.H. (1992). *The reading/writing teacher's companion: Explore poetry.* Portsmouth, NH: Heinemann.

Graves, D.H. (1994). *A fresh look at writing.* Portsmouth, NH: Heinemann.

Harste, J. (1989). *New policy guidelines for reading: Connecting research and practice.* Urbana, IL: National Council of Teachers of English.

Heard, G. (1999). *Awakening the heart: Exploring poetry in elementary and middle school.* Portsmouth, NH: Heinemann.

Henderson, K. (2001). *A young writer's guide to getting published.* Cincinnati, OH: F & W Publications.

Hillocks, G. (1986). *Research on written composition.* Urbana, IL: National Council of Teachers of English.

International Reading Association & National Council of Teachers of English. (1996). *Standards for the English language arts.* Newark, DE: Author; Urbana, IL: Author.

Karolides, N.J. (1999). Theory and practice: An interview with Louise M. Rosenblatt. *Language Arts, 70*(2), 158–169.

Lane, B. (1993). *After the end: Teaching and learning creative revision.* Portsmouth, NH: Heinemann.

Lytle, S., & Botel, M. (1996). *The Pennsylvania framework for reading, writing, and talking across the curriculum.* Harrisburg, PA: Pennsylvania Department of Education.

McVeigh-Schultz, J., & Ellis, M.L. (1997). *With a poet's eye: Children translate the world.* Portsmouth, NH: Heinemann.

Morretta, T.M., & Ambrosini, M. (2000). *Practical approaches for teaching reading and writing in middle school.* Newark, DE: International Reading Association.

Morrow, L.M., & Tracey, D.H. (1997). Strategies used for phonics instruction in early childhood classrooms. *The Reading Teacher, 50,* 644–651.

Myers, M.P. (1997/1998). Passion for poetry. *Journal of Adolescent & Adult Literacy, 41,* 262–270.

National Board for Professional Teaching Standards. (2001). *English language arts standards.* Southfield, MI: Author.

Peterson, R., & Eeds, M. (1990). *Grand conversations: Literature groups in action.* New York: Scholastic.

Robertson, J. (1997). Poetry in science. *Voices From the Middle, 4*(2), 7–10.

Rosenblatt, L.M. (1965). *Literature as exploration.* New York: Modern Language Association of America.

Routmann, R. (1991). *Invitations: Changing as teachers and learners K–12.* Portsmouth, NH: Heinemann.

Sierra-Perry, M. (1996). *Standards in practice: Grades 3–5.* Urbana, IL: National Council of Teachers of English.

Smagorinsky, P. (1996). *Standards in practice: Grades 9–12.* Urbana, IL: National Council of Teachers of English.

Yatvin, J. (1991). Developing a whole language program for a whole school. Newark, DE: International Reading Association & Virginia State Reading Association.

Zemelman, S., Daniels, H., & Hyde, A. (1998). *Best practice: New standards for teaching and learning in America's schools.* Portsmouth, NH: Heinemann.

POETRY AND LITERATURE REFERENCES

Bagert, B. (Ed.). (1994). *Poetry for young people: Edgar Allen Poe*. New York: Sterling.

Bambara, T.C. (1994). The war of the wall. In *Language and literature*. Evanston, IL: McDougal, Littell.

Barnes & Noble Books (Ed.). (1993). Poem 27: I'm nobody. Who are you? In *The Collected Poems of Emily Dickinson*. New York: Editor.

Baylor, B. (1989). *Amigo*. New York: Aladdin.

Beals, M. (1994). *Warriors don't cry: A searing memoir of the battle to integrate Little Rock's Central High School*. New York: Pocket Star.

Berry, J.R. (1997). *Everywhere faces everywhere: Poems*. New York: Simon & Schuster.

Bolin, F. (Ed.). (1984). *Poetry for young people: Emily Dickinson*. New York: Sterling.

Brett, J. *Annie and the wild animals*. Boston: Houghton Mifflin.

Fleischman, P. (1988). *Joyful noise: Poems for two voices*. New York: HarperCollins.

Fletcher, R. (1997). *Ordinary things: Poems from a walk in early spring* (Walter Lyon Krudop, Ill.). New York: Atheneum.

Friedrich, E. (1999). *Leah's pony*. Honesdale, PA: Boyds Mills Press.

Haskins, J. (1993). *Get on board: The story of the underground railroad*. New York: Scholastic.

Hughes, L. (1996). *The Dream Keeper and other poems* (Brian Pinkney, Ill.). New York: Knopf.

Khalsa, D.K. (1999). *I want a dog*. Toronto: Tundra.

King, M.L., Jr. (1963). *I have a dream*. Atlanta, GA: Estate of Dr. Martin Luther King, Jr.

Krause, T. (2001). *Touching hearts—Touching greatness: Stories from a coach that touch your heart and inspire your soul*. Kansas City: Andrews McMeel.

Maxner, J. (1991). *Lady Bugatti*. New York: Lothrop Lee & Shepard.

Orwell, G. (1990). *Animal farm*. San Diego: Harcourt. (Originally published 1945)

Osofsky, A. (1994). *My buddy*. New York: Henry Holt.

Pollette, N. (1989). *The little old woman and the hungry cat*. New York: Greenwillow.

Rawls, W. (1984). *Where the red fern grows*. New York: Random House. (Originally published 1961)

Schmidt, G.D. (Ed.). (1994). *Poetry for young people: Robert Frost*. New York: Sterling.

Schoonmaker, F. (Ed.). (1998). *Poetry for young people: Henry Wadsworth Longfellow*. New York: Sterling.

Silverstein, S. (1996). *Falling up*. New York: HarperCollins.

Soto, G. (1995). *New and selected poems by Gary Soto*. San Francisco: Chronicle.

Taylor, T. (1987). *The cay*. New York: Random House. (Originally published 1969)

Thayer, E. (2000). *Casey at the bat: A ballad of the republic sung in the year 1888*. New York: Handprint Books. (Originally published 1888)

Trapani, I. (1999). *My Jack*. Watertown, MA: Charlesbridge.

Viorst, J. (1976). *The tenth good thing about Barney*. New York: Aladdin.

Wood, A. (1984). *The napping house*. San Diego: Harcourt.

MUSICAL REFERENCES

Beethoven, L. (2001). Symphony No. 9. Song of joy. Second movement; molto vivace [Performed by Arthur Grumiaux, Vladimir Ashkenazy et al.]. On *Essential Beethoven* [CD]. New York: PolyGram Records.

Brown, J., Starks, J., & Bobbit, C. (1995). Pass the peas [Recorded by The J.B.'s]. On The J.B.'s: *Funky good time: The anthology* [CD]. New York: PolyGram Records.

Gershwin, G. (1994). Rhapsody in blue [Performed by Sylvia Capova & Slavonic Philharmonic Orchestra]. On *Classical music for people who hate classical music* [CD]. Roswell, GA: Intersound.

Gershwin, G., & Gershwin, I. (1991). Fascinating rhythm [Performed by Dave Grusin & friends]. On *Dave Grusin: The Gershwin connection* [CD]. New York: GRP Records.

Innes, A., Young, R., Gillespie, B., & Duffy, M. (1996). Trainspotting [Recorded by Primal Fear]. On *Trainspotting* [CD]. London: EMI Records.

Khachaturian, A. (1994). Sabre dance [Performed by Houston Symphony Orchestra]. On *Classical music for people who hate classical music* [CD]. Roswell, GA: Intersound.

Tchaikovsky, P. (1994). Dance of the sugar-plum fairy from The Nutcracker [Recorded by London Festival Orchestra]. On *Classical music for people who hate classical music* [CD]. Roswell, GA: Intersound.

COPYRIGHT ACKNOWLEDGMENTS

Katz, B. (1989). Conversation With a Kite. Copyright ©1989 Random House. Reprinted with permission of Bobbi Katz.

Krause, T. (2001). "Just Me." In *Touching Hearts—Touching Greatness: Stories From a Coach That Touch Your Heart and Inspire Your Soul*. Kansas City: Andrews McMeel. With kind permission of Tom Krause.

Hughes, L. (1994). "I, Too." In *The Collected Poems of Langston Hughes*. Copyright © 1994 by the Estate of Langston Hughes. Used by permission of Alfred A. Knopf. Random House.

Hughes, L. (1994). "Mother to Son." In *The Collected Poems of Langston Hughes*. Copyright © 1994 by the Estate of Langston Hughes. Used by permission of Alfred A. Knopf. Random House.

Silverstein, S. (1996). "No Grown-Ups." In *Falling Up*. Copyright ©1996 by Shel Silverstein. Used by permission of HarperCollins Publishers.

Silverstein, S. (1996). "Scale." In *Falling Up*. Copyright ©1996 by Shel Silverstein. Used by permission of HarperCollins Publishers.

Soto, G. (1995). "The Space." In *New and Selected Poems*. San Francisco: Chronicle Books. Used with permission of Chronicle Books LLC, San Francisco. www.chroniclebooks.com

Whitman, W. (c1900). *Leaves of Grass*. Philadelphia: David McKay.

INDEX

References followed by *f* indicate figures.